The New York Times

CROSSWORDS FOR THE HOLIDAYS

LIGHT AND EASY PUZZLES

Edited by
Will Shortz

ST. MARTIN'S GRIFFIN 🙞 NEW YORK

THE NEW YORK TIMES CROSSWORDS FOR THE HOLIDAYS.
 For information, address St. Martin's Press, 175 Fifth Avenue, New York, N.Y. 10010.

www.stmartins.com

ISBN 0-312-30603-2

First Edition: October 2002

10 9 8 7 6 5 4 3 2 1

The New York Times

CROSSWORDS FOR THE HOLIDAYS

LIGHT AND EASY PUZZLES

1

by Fred Piscop

ACROSS

1. Understood
4. Some tracks
9. ___ Rizzo ('69 Hoffman role)
14. Santa ___ winds
15. Actress Anouk
16. Significant person?
17. Kauai keepsake
18. Small person
20. Legit
22. Caroline Schlossberg, to Ted Kennedy
23. Type style: Abbr.
24. Big Mama
25. Church part
29. Rummy variety
32. The mark on the C in Čapek
33. Calendar period, to Kirk
37. Caustic substance
38. Traditional tune
40. Pub quaff
42. Logical newsman?
43. Long-lasting curls
45. Depicts
49. Health-food store staple
50. Jerry Herman composition
53. Dash
54. Michelangelo masterpiece
56. Journalist Greeley
58. Used booster cables
62. Tina's ex
63. Correspond, grammatically
64. Regarded favorably
65. Pince-___
66. Former Justice Byron
67. Air-show maneuvers
68. Palindrome center

DOWN

1. French
2. ___ time (singly)
3. Taipei's land
4. Honolulu locale
5. Fat fiddle
6. Fuse word
7. First name in hotels
8. Big rigs
9. Campus mil. grp.
10. Daughter of Zeus
11. Calendar abbr.
12. Theology sch.
13. Eye
19. ___ man (flunky)
21. Hooch container
24. Magna ___
26. Rights grp.
27. "Oy ___!"
28. ___ out (supplement)
30. Hoosegows
31. Footrace terminus
32. Stage actress Hayes
34. MS follower?
35. Love, Italian style
36. Newcastle-upon-, England
38. Esne
39. Judge's exhortation
40. Prone
41. Name of 13 popes
44. Oscar the Grouch, for one
46. Julia Louis-Dreyfus on "Seinfeld"
47. Pool-ball gatherer
48. Common cause for blessing
50. Strawberry, once
51. "Any Time ___" (Beatles tune)
52. Auto-racer Andretti
55. Words of comprehension
56. "David Copperfield" character
57. Ten to one, e.g.
58. Gossip
59. "That's disgusting!"
60. High-tech med. diagnostics
61. Foreman stat

by Sidney L. Robbins

ACROSS

1. New Woman rival
5. One-liners
9. Soccer legend
13. Egg-shaped
14. TV oldie "Green ___"
16. Vientiane's land
17. Building code requirement
19. Prod
20. Pilgrim John
21. Most pleasant
23. Madam's mate
25. July 4, 1776, e.g.
26. Opposite of vert.
29. W. Hemisphere org.
32. Mr. Arnaz
34. The lowdown on dancing?
36. Kind of car or sandwich
38. Use a crayon
41. Ratted (on)
42. Armbone
43. By oneself
44. Writer Hunter
45. Hauls
46. Stimulate, as curiosity
47. Measure out
48. Provence city
50. Stalin ruled it
52. "The Bridge of San Luis ___"
53. Stephen of "The Crying Game"
54. Late tennis V.I.P.
57. Dawn goddess
59. Lustrous fabric
61. "Faust," for one
65. [Shock!]
67. Summer treat
70. Matures
71. Go 1–1 in a doubleheader
72. Letterman's "Top Ten," e.g.
73. Model's position
74. "Auld Lang ___"
75. Not so much

DOWN

1. Divan
2. "Hear no ___ . . ."
3. Cooking fat
4. Hightails it
5. Oil alternative
6. U.N.C. and U.Va. grp.
7. In a lofty style
8. Artist's brown
9. +
10. Bulldozer
11. Captain's record
12. Language suffix
15. Church offshoot
18. Arthurian lady
22. Slippery one
24. Sum up
27. Not quite spherical
28. Los Angeles motorist King
29. Of the eyes
30. Magnetism
31. Shades
33. By oneself: Prefix
35. News entry
37. Home port
39. Burden
40. Hall-of-Famer Pee Wee
49. Was in session
51. Motel vacancy
55. Does needlework
56. Mounds
58. "How do you ___ relief?"
60. Church nook
62. Writer Wiesel
63. Flagmaker Betsy
64. Picnic pests
65. Cumberland, e.g.
66. In the past
68. One for Wilhelm
69. Numbered rd.

1	2	3	4	■	5	6	7	8	■	■	9	10	11	12
13				■	14				15	■	16			
17				18						■	19			
20					■	■	21			22			■	■
■	■	■	23		24	■	25				■	26	27	28
29	30	31	■	32		33		■	■	34	35			
36			37	■	38			39	40	■	41			
42				■	43					■	44			
45				■	46					■	47			
48				49	■	■	50			51	■	52		
53			■	54	55	56		■	57		58	■	■	■
■	■	59	60					■	■	61		62	63	64
65	66			■	67			68	69					
70				■	71					■	72			
73				■	■	74				■	75			

by Peter Gordon

ACROSS

1. Like Ike
5. Wellesley student
9. One 39-Across
13. "I cannot tell ___"
14. Heraldic band
15. Sandbags, maybe
16. Holds up
17. Café additive
18. Chemically nonreactive
19. Chiffonier
21. One 39-Across
23. One 39-Across
25. Verboten: Var.
26. Cantankerous
32. Rep.'s rival
35. "___ be a cold day in Hell . . ."
38. Ancient region of Asia Minor
39. Each of eight in this puzzle
43. Like measles
44. Elliptical
45. Compass dir.
46. Home to Denali National Park
48. Teases
51. One 39-Across
56. One 39-Across
60. Stay informed
62. Island group near Fiji
63. Periodical of haute couture
65. Small dog breed, for short
66. One 39-Across
67. Plaintiff
68. Get ready
69. Fusses
70. Orly birds?
71. Lighten up

DOWN

1. Fishhook part
2. One way to read
3. Sign of autumn's beginning
4. Go AWOL
5. One 39-Across
6. ___ pro nobis
7. Statesman Root
8. Coup ___
9. Clinton Transportation Secretary Federico ___
10. Penultimate fairy tale word
11. Wonk, maybe
12. Pocket
15. Actress Ullmann
20. One-time link
22. Symbol for density
24. Expenditure
27. Singer Ocasek of the Cars
28. Classic drama of Japan
29. Seth's son
30. Ocho ___, Jamaica
31. One 39-Across
32. 1982 movie thriller
33. Iniquitous
34. Pianist Hess
36. Broadway comedy of 1964
37. Live's partner
40. ___ Palmas (Canary Islands seaport)
41. Benevolent guy
42. Macs
47. King Kong, e.g.
49. Quilt-making gathering
50. Treeless plain
52. Like the Boston-accented pronunciation of many words
53. Card catalogue abbr.
54. Where the fat lady sings
55. Zaps
56. Ask to produce proof of age
57. Melville novel
58. Participates in a regatta, perhaps
59. One of the Bobbsey twins
61. ___ Le Pew
62. Loan-granting Fed. agcy.
64. Fill a flat?

by Thomas W. Schier

ACROSS

1. Canyon sound
5. Cross-legged exercises
9. August forecast
14. Bumbler
15. 50–50
16. Mohawk Valley city
17. Kitchen fat
18. Shea Stadium nine
19. Pressed one's luck
20. Big eared animal
21. Vacation locale
23. In ___ (ready for release)
25. Sign of summer
26. Cordage
29. It's on page 77
34. Gerald Ford's birthplace
36. Banned apple spray
38. By way of
39. Vacation locale
42. Declare
43. Congressman Gingrich
44. Solemn procedures
45. "___ forget"
47. 1959 Fiestas song
49. Comic Charlotte
51. Outcome
54. Vacation locale
60. Have a tab
61. Like gold
62. On-the-cob treat
63. Ilsa of "Casablanca"
64. Wrist movement
65. Tale starter
66. Pre-owned
67. Army vehicles (You're welcome!)
68. Blue-green
69. Jolly, to the British

DOWN

1. Brilliance
2. Sharply disagree
3. Monmouth Park events
4. ___ man out
5. Sana native
6. "Back to you"
7. Fetches
8. Photographer Adams
9. Rock of Hollywood
10. Jazz locale
11. Muralist Joan
12. Cake decorator
13. Janet Reno's home county
21. Lacquer
22. Pine
24. Associate
27. Put the finger on
28. Is brilliant
30. Painter's mishaps
31. Russian parliament building
32. Sea swooper
33. "Broom Hilda" creator Myers
34. Whitish gem
35. Military command?
37. "Wheels"
40. Late-late show hour
41. Vacation events
46. Violent downfalls
48. Tornado part
50. Orlando attraction
52. Shareholder
53. Sleepwear item
54. ___-Hartly Act
55. Hip-shaking in Kauai
56. Actress Moran
57. Rube
58. TV knob
59. Whale of a movie
63. Broadway hit of 1964–65

by Norma Steinberg

ACROSS

1. "Shane" star
5. Late actor Phoenix
10. "Dark Lady" singer, 1974
14. "___ in a manger . . ."
15. Author Zola
16. "___ from New York . . ."
17. Haircuts?
19. Kathleen Battle offering
20. "___ we having fun yet?"
21. Glowing
22. Kuwaiti structure
24. Opening word
26. Broadway show based on a comic strip
27. Dubuque native
29. Imperturbable
33. Become frayed
36. Former spouses
38. Conceited smile
39. Hawkeye portrayer
40. Recording auditions
42. Garfield's canine pal
43. Pilots let them down
45. Cushy
46. Catches some Z's
47. It fugits
49. Gullible
51. Sufficient
53. Knucklehead
57. Horoscope heading
60. Police blotter abbr.
61. Prospector's find
62. World rotator?
63. Fake embroidery?
66. Augury
67. "This way in" sign
68. ___ carotene
69. Emcee Parks
70. Nursery packets
71. Flowery verses

DOWN

1. Actor Lorenzo
2. Conscious
3. Odense residents
4. Recolor
5. Critiqued
6. ". . . ___ a man with seven wives"
7. ___ ordinaire
8. "Candle in the Wind" singer ___ John
9. Copal and others
10. Vandalized art work?
11. Put on staff
12. Heinous
13. Kind of estate
18. Movie Tarzan ___ Lincoln
23. Whoppers
25. Smog?
26. Showy flower
28. Lumber camp implements
30. Verdi heroine
31. Stumble
32. Makes do, with "out"
33. Float
34. Madame's pronoun
35. Eden resident
37. Divan
41. Scoundrels
44. Its usefulness goes to waste
48. Cumin and cardamom
50. Test tube
52. Actor Greene
54. Courted
55. Livid
56. Ann Richards's bailiwick
57. Poor fellow
58. "Be our guest!"
59. Concluded
60. Thunderstruck
64. Part of a year in Provence
65. Cable add-on

1	2	3	4	■	5	6	7	8	9	■	10	11	12	13
14				■	15					■	16			
17				18						■	19			
20			■	21			■	22		23				
24			25			■	26					■	■	■
■	■	■	27			28		■	29			30	31	32
33	34	35		■	36			37	■	38				
39				■	40				41	■	42			
43				44	■	45				■	46			
47					48	■	49			50		■	■	■
■	■	■	51			52		■	53			54	55	56
57	58	59					■	60			■	61		
62				■	63		64				65			
66				■	67					■	68			
69				■	70					■	71			

6

by Joel Davajan

ACROSS

1. Atop
5. Clubbed
10. Motes
14. New York Cosmos star
15. Chou ___
16. Oklahoma tribesman
17. Lord Nelson site
20. Part of an electrical switch
21. Zeroes
22. Hectored
23. Sans verve
24. Medicament
27. Winter woe
28. Ottoman official
31. The Donald's ex
32. Fly like Lindbergh
33. Aits in Arles
34. Prepare for an Indian attack
37. Raison d'___
38. 30's actress Grey and others
39. Nighttime noise
40. Beam
41. Sponsorship
42. Feeds a furnace
43. Belgian river
44. Baseball union boss Donald
45. Like llamas
48. Sends quickly
52. Ships' drop-off location?
54. Sea flyer
55. Gnawed away
56. Composition closure
57. Crazy bird?
58. Monopoly payments
59. Formerly

DOWN

1. Goes (for)
2. ___ Beach, Fla.
3. Airline to Jerusalem
4. Testimonial
5. It's hummed
6. 1973 hit by the Rolling Stones
7. Covered
8. The "E" in E.N.T.
9. Prohibit
10. Wampum
11. I-70's western terminus
12. Ilk
13. Golf course 18
18. Of some electrodes
19. Printer's spacer
23. Tree trunks
24. Potato preparer
25. "Requiem for ___" (Broadway song)
26. Take the plunge
27. Lawyer Roy M. and others
28. "Take ___ at this!"
29. Type
30. Bridge of ___ (Euclid proposition)
32. Way up?
33. Blissful state?
35. Produce
36. Wheezing cause
41. Birthright seller
42. TV listing
43. Modern-day Sheba
44. Tops
45. Ex-steelworkers chief
46. Fiery fiddler
47. 1962 Bond villain
48. Solar disk
49. Mr. Stravinsky
50. Lawyers' degrees
51. Install in office
53. "___ you sure?"

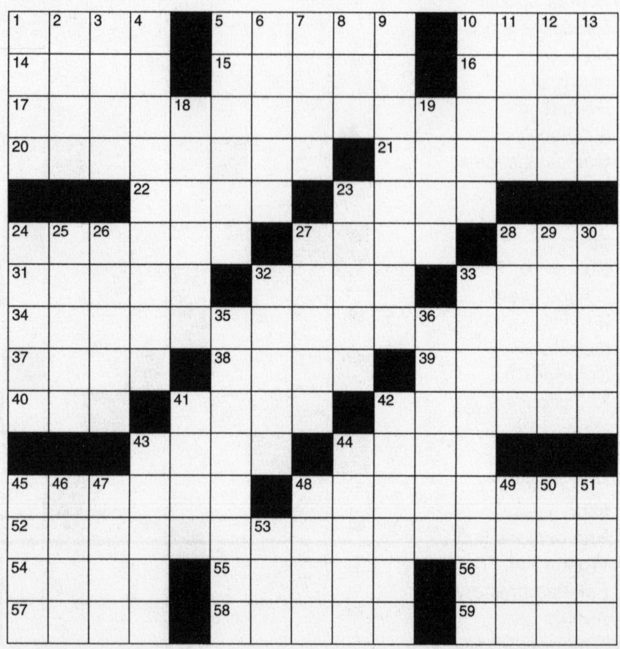

by Sidney L. Robbins

ACROSS

1. Gore's "___ in the Balance"
6. One who's "agin" it
10. Train unit
13. "___ Without Windows" ('64 song)
14. Supermarket meat label
15. Territory
16. Major Bowes updated?
18. Fat
19. Home on the range
20. Kind of signal
21. Part of SEATO
22. Mail HQ
23. Breakfast order
25. Lift up
29. Woodworker's choice
32. Belgian airline
34. Bests
38. Hemingway opus
41. Dub again
42. Took ten
43. Ingenious
45. Shows remorse
46. Up
50. Marinaro and others
52. Slough
53. Reckon
56. Bosom companions
60. "Remember the neediest," e.g.
61. Olympia Dukakis film
63. Fast time
64. Capri, for one
65. Misrepresent
66. Pupil's place
67. African lake
68. Volvo worker

DOWN

1. Bridge seat
2. Comic Johnson
3. Imitation morocco
4. Civil wrong
5. ___ Pinafore
6. Cottonwoods
7. Grammy-winning pianist
8. Yacht heading
9. Person of will
10. 1929 event
11. High nest
12. "M*A*S*H" character
15. "Too bad!"
17. Parapsychology study
22. Authentic
24. Singing sisters
25. D.C. zone
26. Comic Bert
27. Have ___ in one's bonnet
28. Probe
30. Flat sign?
31. Vienna is its cap.
33. In opposition to one another
35. River to the Seine
36. Town near Padua
37. Osmose
39. Melmachian of TV
40. 80's org.
44. Craved
46. With room to spare
47. "Little Orphan Annie" poet
48. Goodnight girl
49. Pants part
51. ___ Plaines
54. Deluxe
55. Southeast Kansas town
56. Witch's ___
57. Golden, e.g.
58. Tart
59. ___ Ball (arcade game)
62. Kitchen meas.

1	2	3	4	5	■	6	7	8	9	■	■	10	11	12
13					■	14				■	15			
16					17					■	18			
19				■	20					■	21			
■	■	■	■	22			■	■	23	24				
25	26	27	28		■	29	30	31			■	■	■	■
32					33	■	34				35	36	37	■
38						39								40
■	41							■	42					
■	■	■	■	43				44	■	45				
46	47	48	49			■	■	50	51		■	■	■	■
52				■	53	54	55			■	56	57	58	59
60				■	61					62				
63				■	64				■	65				
66			■	■	67				■	68				

8

by Randolph Ross

ACROSS

1. Like Job
8. Bob or beehive
14. Leisurely musical pieces
15. Decrees
17. Pentagon advocate?
19. Parlor piece
20. Ex-Knick coach Jackson
21. Author of "Life in London"
22. Heart of France
24. Part
25. Visit Elaine L. Chao?
31. Medical apprentice
32. Ease
37. Blue "Yellow Submarine" characters
38. Revised
40. Ancient beginning
41. Off course
42. Foggy Bottom boat?
46. Narc's collar
50. "Since ___ Have You"
51. Not for
52. Juan's uncle
53. Pescadores neighbor
59. Attorney General's piano practice?
62. Tympanic membrane
63. Guides, in a way
64. Brews tea
65. Menu listings

DOWN

1. Falsifies accounts
2. Chick ender
3. White House heavyweight
4. Beach Boys' "___ Around"
5. "___ kleine Nachtmusik"
6. Titan tip
7. Poetic monogram
8. Spa installation
9. Maestro Toscanini
10. Words often exchanged
11. Twice as unlikely
12. Down Under dog
13. "Love Story" star
16. January 1 song ending
18. Riding the waves
23. Bullfight cries
25. Walk with difficulty
26. Unwanted classification, once
27. Printing style: Abbr.
28. Hawaiian state bird
29. Kingston and others
30. Fee schedule
33. Friend of Ernie
34. Sills solo
35. Caterpillar construction
36. Advantage
38. Calling company
39. Intersection maneuver
43. Asks for a loan
44. They trip up foreigners
45. Magician's sound effect
46. First or home, e.g.
47. Last of the Mohicans
48. Genesis
49. Spanish squiggle
54. ___ were (so to speak)
55. Ovid's way
56. Oenologist's interest
57. Entr'___
58. Costner character
60. Prior, to Prior
61. G.I. ___

by Sidney L. Robbins

ACROSS

1. Hearth debris
6. Atmosphere
10. Columnist Bombeck
14. Room to ___
15. Skater Heiden
16. High time?
17. Critical juncture
20. Parade
21. Some oranges
22. Roasting items
25. Sometimes they get the hang of it
26. Woolly one
30. Carnegie Hall event
32. Where Marco Polo traveled
33. Tomb tenant
34. All fired up?
37. Future brass
41. Modeled, maybe
42. Mountain ridge
43. Peruvian of yore
44. Neptune's fork
46. Physicist Niels
47. Work, work, work
49. Its password was "Mickey Mouse"
51. Trotsky rival
52. Straight shooters?
57. Stops rambling
61. Algerian seaport
62. Broadway groom of 1922
63. Sister of Thalia
64. Bridge seat
65. Bank holding
66. Prepare to shave

DOWN

1. Cleo's snakes
2. Flyspeck
3. "Let the Sunshine In" musical
4. Sea bird
5. Bristles
6. W.W. I grp.
7. Mausoleum item
8. "Road to ___
9. Beginnings of poetry?
10. Involve
11. Beauty aid
12. Folkways
13. Writer Beattie and others
18. Poet translated by FitzGerald
19. Toledo locale
23. Depended
24. Perfumed
26. Senate output
27. On the briny
28. "Gorillas in the ___"
29. Hit a fly, perhaps
31. Mean
34. Host Jay
35. Yen
36. Ivan, for one
38. Church front area
39. Expensive rug
40. Fish in a way
44. Aptitude
45. Weight allowance
47. Pack away
48. "Falcon Crest" star
50. "Egad!"
51. Barge
53. McHenry, e.g.
54. Münchhausen, for one
55. Within: Prefix
56. Common sign
58. Sash
59. Cause for overtime
60. Clucker

by Janie Lyons

ACROSS

1. Child's getaway
5. Nurse's stick
9. Malpractice target
14. Margarine
15. Part of a cash register
16. Sam or Tom, e.g.
17. Businessperson's oxymoron
20. Crowbar
21. Runner Devers
22. Sums
23. "Get ___!"
25. Cut up
27. Vipers
30. Indignant person's oxymoron
35. Actor Erwin
36. Breezy
37. Refer (to)
38. Dinner bird
40. Command to Fido
42. Jewish dinner
43. Mideast language
45. Flood survivor
47. W.W. II grp.
48. Oxymoron for a homely person
50. Cheek
51. Riches' opposite
52. Took a powder
54. Jacob's brother
57. Bare
59. Speechify
63. Coffee drinker's oxymoron
66. Passé
67. Within: Prefix
68. Model married to David Bowie
69. Steeple
70. Slumber
71. Library item

DOWN

1. Monk's hood
2. Lotion ingredient
3. Former talk-show host
4. Fireplace equipment
5. Penn, e.g.: Abbr.
6. Belly dancers
7. Edison's middle name
8. Mathematician Pascal
9. Sine ___ non
10. Straighten out
11. Sarcasm
12. Dolt
13. Barbies' mates
18. Enrage
19. Bow of silents
24. Black bird
26. Three-time Super Bowl-winning coach
27. Tin Pan Alley org.
28. One of the Beatles
29. Chrysalises
31. In competition
32. Lindley of "The Ropers"
33. Creativity
34. Indoor balls
36. Writer Loos
39. Busybody
41. Stashes
44. Caesar's swans
46. Certain vote
49. Shylock
50. Magellan, e.g.
53. Lee to Grant
54. Concludes
55. It's seen in bars
56. Against
58. Unit of force
60. BB's
61. Word after "go!"
62. Sea eagle
64. Humorist George
65. "Oh, darn!"

1	2	3	4	■	5	6	7	8	■	9	10	11	12	13
14				■	15				■	16				
17				18					19					
20					■	21				■	22			
■	■	■	23		24		■	25		26		■	■	■
27	28	29		■	30		31					32	33	34
35			■	36				■	37					
38			39		■	40		41	■	42				
43					44	■	45		46		■	47		
48						49				■	50			
■	■	■	51				■	52		53		■	■	■
54	55	56		■	57		58		■	59		60	61	62
63				64					65					
66					■	67				■	68			
69					■	70				■	71			

by Janet R. Bender

ACROSS

1. Wrongs
5. Stockyard group
9. Sail supports
14. Govt. agents
15. War of 1812 battle site
16. Member of a crowd scene
17. Give stars to
18. Basketball's Chamberlain
19. 1993 Formula One winner Prost
20. Old "House Party" host
23. Knocks down
24. Reserved
25. 1975 Stephanie Mills musical, with "The"
28. Hot time in Paris
29. Take turns
33. Kind of package
34. More albinolike
35. Phobic
37. P.G.A.'s 1992 leading money winner
39. Rickey Henderson stat
41. Hunter of myth
42. Well ventilated
43. Least exciting
45. Rotary disk
48. Sign of summer
49. Mathematician's letters
50. Throw
52. N.F.L. receiver for 18 seasons
57. Booby
59. Not in use
60. Crips or Bloods
61. Uris's "___ Pass"
62. Baylor mascot
63. Skirt
64. Check writer
65. Slumped
66. Actress Charlotte et al.

DOWN

1. Attack by plane
2. Turkish hostelry
3. Stinging plant
4. Fish-line attachment
5. Axed
6. Dancer Bruhn
7. Small brook
8. Loathe
9. Substantial
10. Wheel shaft
11. Noted film trilogy
12. Angle starter
13. ___ Jose
21. Hebrew for "contender with God"
22. Eponymous poet of Greek drama
26. Temper
27. British alphabet ender
30. Elderly one
31. Gumshoe
32. "___ With a View"
33. Columnist Herb
34. Supplicate
36. Thread of life spinner, in myth
37. Savageness
38. Late actress Mary
39. NaCl, to a pharmacist
40. Truss
44. Deviates from the script
45. Party to NAFTA
46. Exact retribution
47. Enters a freeway
49. Persian Gulf land
51. Trevanian's "The ___ Sanction"
53. Green target
54. Madison Avenue product
55. Ardor
56. Boor
57. Cutup
58. Noche's opposite

by Sidney L. Robbins

ACROSS

1. Wealthy person
5. Takes advantage of
9. "The Forsyte ___"
13. Likeness
15. Kind of stick
16. Sheriff Tupper of "Murder, She Wrote"
17. Social hangout
19. Sea swallow
20. Home turnover
21. Knock out of kilter
23. Illuminated
24. Terminator
25. Bear up there
29. Steep slope
33. Crier of Greek myth
35. Wakens
39. Bettor's challenge
43. Show fright
44. Weird
45. Followed orders
48. N.Y. Police ___
49. Exodus priest
53. Mauna ___
55. Responded unintelligibly
58. "Last stop!"
62. Abner's pal and namesakes
63. Diamond coup
66. Relative of the flute
67. Auction actions
68. Indian boat
69. Part of Halloween makeup
70. Church nook
71. Endure

DOWN

1. Informal greetings
2. Eastern V.I.P.
3. Wind instrument?
4. They'll be hunted in April
5. Big sports news
6. Loudly weep
7. "Holy moly!"
8. Kind of loser
9. Beelzebub
10. Change
11. Watkins Glen, e.g.
12. "Lou Grant" star
14. Lod airport airline
18. Nobelist Wiesel
22. Esteem
25. German link
26. Kind of squad
27. Lemonlike
28. Singer Lane
30. Cuomo's predecessor
31. Son of Prince Valiant
32. Australian hopper
34. Long Island town
36. Tool storage area
37. Limerick site
38. Barber's cut
40. Wane
41. Bullring shout
42. Receive
46. Pass
47. Cabbage Patch item
49. Visibly happy
50. Caribbean getaway
51. "___ has it . . ."
52. Start
54. Actor Guinness
56. Old lab burner
57. Trapdoor
59. Milky gem
60. Arm bone
61. Pueblo town
64. Employee card and others
65. Still and all

by Nancy Joline

ACROSS

1. More exuberant, as a laugh
5. Snatch
9. "Cold hands, ___"
14. Mast-steadying rope
15. Hitchcock's "___ Window"
16. Of a region
17. Now's partner
18. Eggshell Color
19. Rubberneck
20. Altar in the sky
21. Sault ___ Marie
22. Yarmulke
24. Capts.' subordinates
25. Campaign donor grp.
26. Some bikes
28. "___ the season . . ."
29. Upper regions of space
31. Scrabble piece
32. Mare's offspring
33. Judged
35. Place for E.M.K.
36. Concordes land there
37. Without reservation
40. Little demon
43. Corn site
44. Prolonged attacks
48. Steak order
49. Vesuvius's Sicilian counterpart
51. Boston Garden, e.g.
52. Gametes
53. Theater aide
55. White House defense grp.
56. Barbie's beau
57. Sixth sense
58. Joad and Kettle
59. Wilder's "___ Town"
60. Singer John
62. Gibbons
64. Desiccated
65. Means of connection
66. Gambler's "bones"
67. Like some cars
68. Pulse indication
69. Collectors' goals
70. February 14 symbol

DOWN

1. Like some candy boxes
2. Repeat
3. Otalgia
4. Place for ham and Swiss
5. Miss Garbo
6. Modern
7. Swiss river
8. Movie star with a kick?
9. Ethnic group portrayed in A. R. Gurney's plays
10. ___ Deco
11. Person who can move buildings
12. Kind of arts or law
13. With cruelty
21. ___ throat
23. Alters
27. Discourages
30. Overact
32. Where to go between acts
34. Restrains
38. Reporters' needs
39. Tale tellers
40. Jilted lover's woe
41. Entangler
42. Sanchez Vicario of tennis
45. Columbus, by birth
46. Guaranteed
47. University in Bridgeport, Conn.
50. Mien
53. Slow on the uptake
54. Mitigates
61. Bouncer's demand
63. Pizza
64. California's Big ___

by Harvey Estes

ACROSS

1. Insertion mark
6. Rock layers
12. Kojak portrayer
14. It frequently finds itself in hot water
16. Cracker Jack prize
17. Peter Finch movie "Raid on ___"
18. Saw
19. Chicken ___ king
21. Standing near home, maybe
22. Communion or baptism
23. SALT concern
25. China: Prefix
26. Path for Confucians
27. Language from which "sarong" comes
29. Article in Der Spiegel
30. Hollered
32. "Kon-Tiki" wood
34. Cool, as coffee
35. Computer unit
36. Idiot box
38. Cash reserves
42. Loan org.
43. Beatty's co-star in "Bonnie and Clyde"
45. Paul's singing partner
46. Watermelon waste
48. To ___ mildly
49. Actor John
50. Word with jack or label
52. "I ___ You Babe"
53. Prize money
54. Sugar type
56. Gym exercises
58. Enters helter-skelter
59. Works a deal on
60. Least done
61. Founded

DOWN

1. Of the heart
2. Amelia Earhart, e.g.
3. Roundup site
4. Actress Sommer
5. ___ kwon do
6. X-rated
7. Countdown beginning
8. Pro follower
9. Aids and ___
10. House cats
11. Balkan country
12. Fits' companion
13. Quarterback Ken
15. Divulge
20. Put ammo in
23. Hot-dog
24. Tended tots
27. Became hitched
28. Cooper's Bumppo
31. Superman symbol
33. Grant opponent
35. Enchant like Samantha
36. Where things vanish
37. Absolutely bland
38. Group with HQ in Brussels
39. Debate stifler
40. Understood
41. Underline
42. Dowdy person
44. Guitarist Ted
47. Spoiler
49. Em and Bee
51. Schnozzola
53. Tilting-tower town
55. Mom's girl
57. Spokes' intersection

by Sidney L. Robbins

ACROSS

1. Tot's talk, perhaps
5. Encourages
9. First-grade instruction
13. Stinks
15. "Thanks ___!"
16. Swing around
17. Like factory workers
19. U, for one
20. Elsie's bull
21. "Mommie ___" (Christina Crawford book)
23. "What's ___ for me?"
25. Take a potshot
26. Teller of white lies
29. Stage whisper
30. Give the eye
31. Quick bites
33. Advances
36. Baseball's Gehrig
37. Trunk
39. Runner Sebastian
40. Remains
43. Person of action
44. King's address
45. Illegal inducement
47. Mexican dishes
49. Speak-easy offering
50. Saxophonist Getz
51. Candid
53. Waiter's jotting
56. Actress Archer
57. Kind of jury
61. Bucks and does
62. Otherwise
63. Singer ___ Neville
64. Lawyer: Abbr.
65. Tackle-box item
66. City inside the Servian Wall

DOWN

1. Tennis shot
2. Run in neutral
3. Body's partner
4. Logician's start
5. Sidekick
6. Sum total
7. Wart giver, in old wives' tales
8. Emphasis
9. On a horse
10. Edit
11. No blessing, this!
12. Shipped
14. Fragrance
18. Marco Polo area
22. Dye color appropriate to this puzzle
24. Vacuum tube
26. Go belly up
27. Borodin's prince
28. Texas' State flower
29. Balance-sheet pluses
32. Golf club V.I.P.
34. Illustrator Gustave
35. Comprehends
38. Patrick Henry, e.g.
41. Bodega
42. Clothing specification
44. Boating hazard
46. Saharan tribesman
48. Newswoman Shriver
49. Intelligence-testing name
51. Actress Thompson
52. Glamour rival
54. River of Spain
55. Leeway
58. "It's no ___!"
59. Slippery one
60. Opposite SSW

by Alex K. Justin

ACROSS

1. Dumbfounded
5. Acquire as expenses
10. Singer Campbell
14. Colombian city
15. Hughes's plane Spruce ___
16. 1890's Vice President ___ P. Morton
17. 1959 Rodgers and Hammerstein hit
20. You can ___ horse to . . .
21. Bridal path
22. Predicament
24. Obota's successor
26. 1956 Comden-Green-Styne collaboration
33. On ___ (counting calories)
34. Man with a title
35. Soviet space vehicle
36. Pride and envy, e.g.
37. Old hat
38. "Aurora" painter
39. Kind of cap or cream
40. Radio host of note
41. First U.S. saint
42. 1930 Gershwin musical
46. Stigmatism
47. Achy
48. Whiz kid
51. Blotto
54. 1983 Herman-Fierstein musical
60. "Metamorphoses" poet
61. Wish granters
62. TV's Oscar
63. Hitches
64. Mill material
65. Murder

DOWN

1. Part of a play
2. Star of TV's "Wiseguy"
3. "Waiting for the Robert ___"
4. Puts out of commission
5. Desert critter
6. Persona ___ grata
7. How some packages are sent
8. R. & R. org.
9. Ring leader?
10. Sticking together
11. Decreasingly
12. Demonic
13. Garibaldi's birthplace
18. Keats or Shelley
19. Popular street name
23. Invent
24. Snaps handcuffs on
25. Gentle, as breezes
26. Grounds
27. Kingly decree
28. Passenger ship
29. Gobble
30. "___ man with seven . . ."
31. Curtain material
32. Nine-to-five routine
37. Conks out
38. Mutinied
41. ___ comic (play type)
43. Long narratives
44. Alan, Larry or Stephen
45. Tap-dance
48. Crushing news
49. Four-star review
50. ___ rain
52. Admiral Zumwalt
53. Actress Moore
55. Chicken's counterpart
56. Atmosphere prefix
57. Prefix with lateral
58. Omicrons predecessors
59. Thesaurus listing: Abbr.

by Ernie Furtado

ACROSS
1. Play opening
5. Ran
9. Shawl or afghan
14. Forsaken
15. Yellow brick, e.g.
16. Moonshine
17. Unencumbered
19. Composed
20. Follower of 21-Across?
21. Follower of 20-Across?
22. Small: Suffix
23. Ripped
24. Dems. opposition
27. Proverbial distancer
32. Sleepy Hollow schoolmaster
34. Ampersand
35. Firpo of the ring
36. Folk tales
37. Ship's officers
39. ___ time (never)
40. Upshots
41. Morning hrs.
42. Waffle topping
43. Kind of disease, facetiously
47. Hook shape
48. Alphabet quartet
49. Unmixed, as a drink
51. Character actor George
54. Starts
58. In the thick of
59. Be afraid to offend
60. Hope of Hollywood
61. Manhattan campus
62. Gamblers' game
63. Boorish
64. Some combos
65. Sharp put-down

DOWN
1. ___ Romeo (automobile)
2. Hip
3. De ___ (too much)
4. Words before "red" or "running"
5. Literary sister
6. Give some slack
7. Maneuver slowly
8. White House monogram
9. Block
10. Fun and games
11. Kind of beer
12. Eight, in combinations
13. A question of time
18. Singer Lenya
21. Merchandise
23. Manner of speaking
24. Staff leader
25. University of Maine site
26. TV announcer Don
28. 1980 DeLuise movie
29. Bizarre
30. "Peanuts" character
31. Stock plans providing worker ownership: Abbr.
33. Young 'uns
37. Horace and Thomas
38. BB's
42. Disreputable
44. Some are spitting
45. World cultural agcy.
46. Flirts
50. Stylish Brits
51. Baby powder
52. Poet Khayyám
53. ___ fide
54. Where humuhumunukunukuapuaa might be served
55. Filly or colt
56. Roman marketplaces
57. Quit
59. Abbr. in a mail-order ad

by Sidney L. Robbins

ACROSS

1. Bakery byproduct
6. Went by plane
10. Copied
14. Arizona features
15. Scottish isle
16. Lemon's partner
17. With 36-Across and 55-Across, a sales pitch disclaimer
20. Baden-Baden and others
21. Shea team
22. Eastern V.I.P.
23. Mr. Caesar
24. Ship to ___
25. "Swan Lake," e.g.
29. Tiny bit
31. Not native
32. Printer's employee
33. Printer's measures
36. See 17-Across
39. His wife took a turn for the worse
40. Obsolescent piano key material
41. Bellini opera
42. Hoarder's cry
43. Telescopist's sighting
44. Strength
47. Opponent
48. Xerox competitor
49. "When I was ___ . . ."
51. In ___ of
55. See 17-Across
58. Person 'twixt 12 and 20
59. "The King and I" setting
60. Singer Cara
61. Misses the mark
62. Paddles
63. Waco locale

DOWN

1. Concert hall equipment
2. Harvest
3. Greek mountain
4. Wrestlers' needs
5. Type of cobra
6. Shot
7. Artist's pad?
8. Son of Seth
9. Revolutionary, e.g.
10. "Remember the ___"
11. Heartbroken swain
12. Leno, for one
13. Bucks and does
18. Give forth
19. Indian noblewoman
23. Feeling
24. Suffix with tip or dump
25. Get-out-of-jail money
26. In addition
27. Bit of fluff
28. Mr. Durocher
29. Harden
30. "Sure, why not?"
32. Borodin's "Prince ___"
33. To be, in Paree
34. Secretarial work
35. Burn
37. Confess
38. "___ on your life!"
43. Fashion
44. "60 Minutes" regular
45. Reason out
46. Sentence subjects
47. Country homes
48. Pigeon coop
49. ___ da capo
50. Noted James Earl Jones stage role
51. Entice
52. The holm oak
53. Erupter of 1669
54. Applications
56. G.I. entertainers
57. Command to Fido

by William P. Baxley

ACROSS

1. Artistic skill
6. Card game also called sevens
12. Holed out in two under par
14. Warned
16. English essayist Richard
17. Burglar
18. Cools, as coffee
19. Pumpkin eater of rhyme
21. Summer drink
22. Employee health plan, for short
23. Horse trainer's equipment
25. Black cuckoos
26. Long, long time
28. Like some schools
29. Sweetens the kitty
30. Smart alecks
32. Traffic circle
33. Charlie Brown's "Darn!"
34. Ex-Mrs. Burt Reynolds
35. Charge with gas
38. Adorned
42. Vineyard fruit
43. Kismet
44. Snick's partner
45. Detest
46. Alternative to eggdrop
48. A Gershwin
49. Drunk ___ skunk
50. Analyze a sentence
51. Actor John of TV's "Addams Family"
53. Locale
55. Money-back deal
57. Boot camp denizen
58. Noted family in china manufacture
59. Arabs
60. Cancel the launch

DOWN

1. "L'état ___": Louis XIV
2. Army grub
3. Ripening agent
4. Butler's "The Way of All ___"
5. ___ Aviv
6. Observed Lent
7. Change the hemline
8. ___ do-well
9. "La-la" preceder
10. Home of the '96 Olympics
11. Poorer
13. Arranges strategically
15. Smart
18. Sullivan's "really big" one
20. Summers, in Haiti
24. Sharp
25. Clowning achievements?
27. Mexican shawl
29. Top-flight
31. Arena receipts
32. Drive in Beverly Hills
34. Epistles
35. Shocked
36. Pencil ends
37. Knocking sound
38. Forbids
39. Bootee maker
40. Most Halloweenlike
41. Doyen
43. Smithies
46. Dwindled
47. High-muck-a-muck
50. Fir
52. Prefix with masochism
54. Item of office attire
56. Fuel efficiency rater: Abbr.

by Betty Jorgensen

ACROSS

1. One who reunes
5. Bic or Parker products
9. Lox's partner
14. Computer offering
15. Face shape
16. Shade of white
17. No ifs, ___ or buts
18. Soho so-long
19. Lounges lazily
20. Start of a quip
23. Consumed
24. Israeli airport
25. ___ chango (magician's command)
29. "That was close!"
31. Horror film frightener
34. Oscar de la ___
35. Mimi Sheraton subject
36. Obstinate one
37. Middle of the quip
40. Hor.'s opposite
41. ___ of March
42. French avenue
43. It's north of Calif.
44. Chance ___ (meet accidentally)
45. Not present
46. Columbus univ.
47. One, in Orléans
48. End of the quip
55. His beloved was Beatrice
56. Old newspaper section
57. Hide
59. Rags-to-riches writer
60. Roughneck
61. Bombeck, the columnist
62. Hops brews
63. Sea eagle
64. Cooper's was high

DOWN

1. Internists' org.
2. Give temporarily
3. Remove, as a knot
4. Daydream
5. Spud
6. Dodge
7. European defense grp.
8. Dross
9. Swell, as a cloud
10. Have nothing to do with
11. Course game
12. A Gardner
13. Fleur-de-___
21. Old Nick
22. Coasters
25. Utah city
26. Allude (to)
27. ___ nous
28. Editor's mark
29. Part of NOW
30. Breaks up clods
31. Company B awakener
32. ". . . in tears amid the ___ corn": Keats
33. Ism
35. Rover's playmate
36. Tormé and Gibson
38. Raise the end of
39. Cacophonous tower
44. Does a groomsman's job
45. Whosoever
46. Bewhiskered animal
47. Author Sinclair
48. Fabric texture
49. "Come Back, Little Sheba" playwright
50. Prod
51. Rating a D
52. Aboveboard
53. Florida's Beach
54. Pollster Roper
55. A tiny bit
58. Ecru

by Martin Schneider

ACROSS

1. Expire, as a membership
6. Show hosts, for short
9. Fill
13. Secretary of State Root
14. Dadaist Hans
15. Like Old King Cole
16. Baseball bigwig Bud
17. Assurance
19. Not brand-name
21. Spring blooms
22. Wildebeest
23. Entomological stage
25. Less original
28. Monks and nuns
32. Apartment sign
33. Lebanese symbol
34. Soup container
35. Immense, poetically
36. Mine find
37. Lift the spirits of
39. From ___ Z
40. Most Egyptians
42. Meet official
43. Louvre highlight
45. Insult
46. 1983 Streisand role
47. Scottish denial
48. Value
51. Lethargy
55. Prohibition establishment
57. Chain of hills
59. Country music's Tucker
60. Drunk's problem, with "the"
61. Near Eastern chieftain
62. Bettor's starter
63. Opposite of WNW
64. Pores over

DOWN

1. Broadway's "___ Miz"
2. Words after shake or break
3. Mass
4. Roof worker
5. Noted name in puzzling
6. Biblical trio
7. Fancy term for 5-Down and 15-Down
8. Vacation destination
9. Grad-to-be
10. Liberal ___
11. Corner
12. Potato features
15. Noted name in puzzling
18. Lasso
20. Čapek play
24. Styles
25. It may come in a head
26. Kemo Sabe's companion
27. Crazy as ___
29. "___, I saw . . ."
30. Eroded
31. Dummy Mortimer
33. Slide
38. Cable choice
41. Washer cycle
44. "Roger," at sea
45. ___ for the books
48. Film dog
49. Breadth
50. Faxed
52. Wall Street abbr.
53. Brainstorm
54. Like some cheeses
56. Suffix added to fruit names
58. Speech stumbles

by Nancy Joline

ACROSS

1. Tops of wine bottles
6. Wreak havoc upon
12. Gorge
13. Undergoes again, as an experience
14. Fund-raiser
15. Requiring immediate action
16. Postprandial drinks
18. Dessert pastry
19. ___ hurrah
20. Actor Jannings
22. Chest rattle
23. Brightened
25. Burghoff role on "M*A*S*H"
27. Columbia, vis-à-vis the ocean
28. Entraps
30. Nullifies
32. Hash house sign
34. Info
35. Reduces
38. Glass ingredient
42. Tex- ___ (hot cuisine)
43. DeMille films
45. Exorcist's adversary
46. Elderly
48. Angry to-do
49. Cable TV's C- ___
50. Scuttlebutt
52. Take to court
55. Burst inward
57. Aficionado
58. It stretches across a tennis court
59. Bellyached
60. They may be liquid
61. Tried to catch a conger

DOWN

1. Variety of rummy
2. William Tell and others
3. Prevalent
4. Make a sweater
5. Hunting dog
6. Tyrannosaurus ___
7. Parted company with a horse
8. Good physical health
9. Nothing special
10. Calms
11. Hold in high regard
12. Stay
13. Sojourned
14. Strike alternatives
17. Muscat is its capital
21. Former capital of Nigeria
24. "___ porridge hot . . ."
26. Word before fire or transit
29. Hitchcock's "The Thirty-Nine ___"
31. Hubble, e.g.
33. Cut, as roses
35. Peanuts, e.g.
36. Frees from liability
37. Disfigure
39. Ascribed
40. Like nuts at a chocolatier's
41. French year
42. Boater's haven
44. Plodding person
47. Fellini's "La ___ Vita"
51. Cheer (for)
53. Devoid of moisture
54. The dark force
56. O.R. personnel

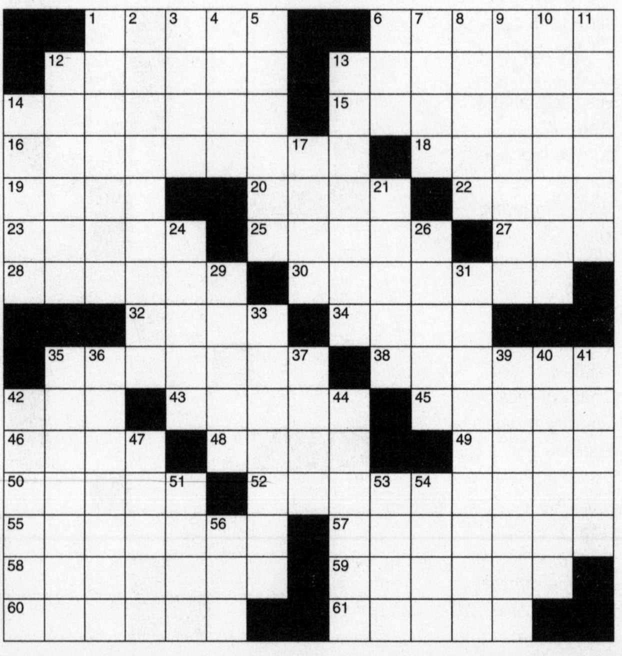

by Bernice Gordon

ACROSS

1. Like some eagles or tires
5. Poker Flat chronicler
10. Price
14. "Now ___ me down . . ."
15. Dillies
16. Patron saint of physicians
17. In need
19. "Miss ___ Regrets"
20. Former Washington nine
21. Journalists Joseph and Stewart
23. Bog
24. Dutch painter Jan
25. Actor Peter
28. Fleet cats
31. Comic Costello
32. ___ incognita
34. Psalms word
35. "Bon" words
37. Appears
39. Flintstones pet
40. Bit of clowning
42. Soup ingredients
44. Cattle call
45. Newborns
47. Shortly
49. End of a tunnel, proverbially
50. Came in horizontally
51. Manhandler
53. Fellow crew member
57. Have an itch for
58. "Fantastic!"
60. 1949 hit "___ in Love With Amy"
61. Sky-hued flower
62. Shoe support
63. Glassmaker's oven
64. Broadcasts
65. Asserts

DOWN

1. Invitations
2. A lily
3. Mowing site
4. Ball of fire
5. Feted ones
6. Tennis's Agassi
7. Collectors' cars
8. Robert Morse stage role
9. Subject of a will
10. Shut up
11. In a tenuous position
12. Leave hastily
13. 1994 film "Guarding ___"
18. Like Pisa's tower
22. Sediment
24. Humiliate
25. Broadway tune "___ River"
26. Ten-___ odds
27. Not with it
28. Northern Indians
29. Vietnam's capital
30. "Darn it!"
33. Rent out again
36. Presaging trouble
38. One-way transporters
41. Zoo fixture
43. Cuts
46. Pulses
48. Owns up to
50. Protected, as the feet
51. Subject to court-martial, maybe
52. Curse
53. Bedaze
54. Taj Mahal site
55. "___ also serve who . . ."
56. Hot times on the Riviera
59. Little: Suffix

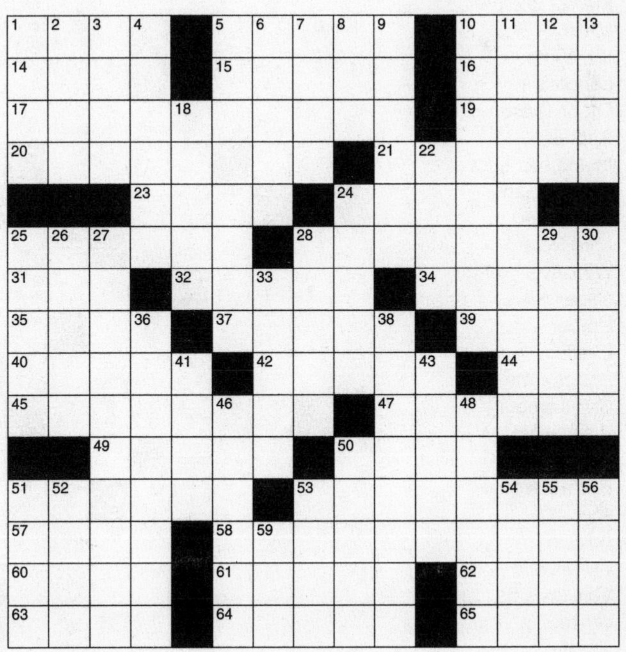

by James L. Beatty

ACROSS

1. Outbuildings
6. Hobgoblin
10. "___ sesame"
14. Mischievous sprite
15. Selves
16. Nuclear reactor
17. Ahead of the times
19. Prefix with marketing
20. Sleep stage
21. Accurate
22. Made an incursion
24. Medicine that's not all it's promised to be
26. Bewails
27. Fictitious
30. Trigonometric function
32. Sashes
33. Oil city of Iran
34. Memorable period
37. Melts
40. It may be penciled in
42. Ott or Gibson
43. Appraised
45. Inland sea east of the Caspian
46. Rephrased
48. Lord Peter Wimsey's creator
50. Caper
52. Uproar
54. Evades
56. ___ of arms
57. Small amount
60. Woodwind instrument
61. Restaurant special
64. Add on
65. Swearword
66. Valletta is its capital
67. Not the pictures
68. Nautical chains
69. Stocking material

DOWN

1. Box
2. Busy place
3. Word with eye or final
4. Gunga ___
5. Resolve
6. ___ Arts
7. Monstrously cruel
8. The Almighty
9. River to the North Sea
10. Right to purchase
11. Secondary residence
12. Actress Burstyn
13. Desiderata
18. Electric power network
23. Astound
24. Noted lioness
25. Take new vows
27. Froth
28. French ecclesiastic
29. Love letter
31. Low island
33. Fall bloomer
35. Bellow
36. Piercing tools
38. Instant
39. ___ one's words
41. Reddish-brown horses
44. Give a little learning
47. Reader's ___
48. Miner's nail
49. Cooling off time
50. Take as one's own
51. Aristocratic
53. Closet pests
55. Espy
57. Kewpie, e.g.
58. Prefix with graph or crat
59. Breakfast fiber source
62. Ballad
63. Blue bird

by Sidney L. Robbins

ACROSS

1. Mosque tops
6. Lone Ranger attire
10. Strike caller
13. Dynamic
14. "I cannot tell ___"
15. Mimic
16. Chinese principles
18. Lavish party
19. Tosspot
20. Worships
21. Freshly
22. Life, for one
23. Enlarge
24. Soup dipper
28. Six-stanza poem
31. Lily
32. Does, for example
33. Knot of hair
36. Procrastinator
40. Relative of the buttercup
42. Moral no-no
43. Tentmaker of fame
45. Kind of camera focus
46. Modified
49. Mount
50. Sighed (for)
52. Playboy pic
54. Took a taxi
55. Sound choice?
57. Busy person around Apr. 15
60. Smidgen that's smashed
61. Occasionally
63. Greek letters
64. Kurdish home
65. Throw out
66. N.Y. winter time
67. Trapper's trophy
68. Fires

DOWN

1. TV's "___ of Our Lives"
2. Hodgepodge
3. Money maker
4. "Uncle Tom's Cabin" girl
5. Spot for 100
6. Giuliani and others
7. Equipped with a theft protector
8. Trig function
9. Barrels
10. No longer bedridden
11. Fracas
12. Shrimp
15. Once more
17. Successor to H.S.T.
23. Telegram
24. Lassies' partners
25. Jai ___
26. Homeless
27. Conducted
29. Melville novel setting
30. Countdown start
34. "Render therefore ___ Caesar . . ."
35. It's a gas
37. Trucker's amount
38. Holy Roman, e.g.: Abbr.
39. Squealer
41. Alluring West
44. License extension
47. Considers
48. "The Story of Civilization" author
49. Hollow stones
50. Jabber
51. Specks
53. Bear's abode
55. Quick cut
56. Ripped
57. In high style
58. Captain Ahab of film
59. Busy ones
62. Initials of 1933

26

by Ed Pegg Jr.

ACROSS

1. "___ Without a Cause"
6. Musical scale letters
11. Joker
14. Smell
15. Of great scope
16. Electric ___
17. Proverb
18. Old-fashioned picture taker
20. Elevator name
22. Victory symbol
23. Norse Zeus
24. Candidate Landon
26. Was sore
28. Having divergent lines
29. Backside
31. DNA shapes
33. Letter getter
35. Seize
36. That lady
39. Make into a spiral
40. Book after Deuteronomy
42. Opposite SSW
43. ___ Mahal
45. 12, at dice
46. Leisurely study
48. Eric of "Monty Python"
49. October gems
52. ___ Rouge
54. Olive ___
55. Sushi go-with
56. National anthem contraction
57. Author Irwin
59. Intercom
62. Smoldering spark
65. Unfashionable
66. "___ a Rainy Night" (1981 hit)
67. On top of
68. Formerly named
69. One of life's certainties, in a saying
70. Deep ___ (discarded)

DOWN

1. Type of computer chip
2. Historical time
3. Ticket booth
4. Discharge
5. Keats poem
6. Recede
7. Beg shamelessly
8. Trapped
9. European freshwater fish
10. Medicine watchdog: Abbr.
11. Uncared for, as a lawn
12. Eagle's nest
13. Liver or thyroid
19. Extinct birds
21. Rhodes ___
24. Jingle writers
25. Greg Evans cartoon
27. Use voodoo on
28. Crate up again
30. ___ Jo, of the '88 Olympics
32. Coaxes
34. Mosquito marks
36. Train for the ring
37. ___-burly
38. Artist's prop
41. ___ fi
44. Diner music maker
45. "Kapow!"
46. Entreaty
47. ___ Tuesday
49. Director Welles
50. Irritate
51. Not obtuse
53. Three-toed birds
56. Neighbor of Ark.
58. Both: Prefix
60. Acumen
61. Illiterates' signatures
63. The day before
64. Ruby

1	2	3	4	5	■	6	7	8	9	10	■	11	12	13
14					■	15					■	16		
17					■	18					19			
■	■	20			21	■	22			■	23			
24	25		■	26		27			■	28				
29			30	■	31				32			■	■	■
33				34			■	35			■	36	37	38
39						■	■	■	40		41			
42			■	43		44	■	45						
■	■	■	46				47			■	48			
49	50	51			■	52				53	■	54		
55				■	56			■	57		58		■	■
59				60				61	■	62			63	64
65			■	66					■	67				
68			■	69					■	70				

by Jonathan Schmalzbach

ACROSS

1. ". . . more than one way to skin ___"
5. Supply a party
10. Beast of burden
13. Fads
15. Speak publicly
16. Caltech rival
17. Cereal "fruit"
19. "___ of these days, Alice . . ."
20. Outdoor
21. Spiritual punishment
23. Meadow
24. Jockey Cordero
25. Civil War flash point
32. Nom de crook
33. Upset
34. Small dog, for short
37. Split
38. Grew ashen
40. Coffee, informally
41. Hat-room fixture
42. Salon offering
43. More painful
44. U.S. commodore in Japan, 1853–54
47. Letter-shaped metal bar
50. Señor Guevara
51. Lovebirds' destination, maybe
54. Paul of "Casablanca"
59. ___ Altos, Calif.
60. County of Northern Ireland
62. Had a little lamb?
63. First name in cosmetics
64. Novelist Françoise
65. Roll of bills
66. Looks (to be)
67. Unattached

DOWN

1. With the bow, in music
2. Bellyache
3. Malarial symptom
4. Part of T.V.A. Abbr.
5. Hooded snakes
6. Exist
7. Diamond cover
8. To be, to Satie
9. "___ the Fox" (classic fable)
10. In the midst of
11. From the time of
12. Girder material
14. ___ of justice
18. Yesterday: Fr.
22. "___ luck?"
25. David's instrument
26. Downwind, nautically
27. Wedding sine qua non
28. Add to, unnecessarily
29. Smut
30. Prior to, in poems
31. Crimson
34. Henry VIII's VIth
35. "Reply completed," to a ham operator
36. Queen of Scots
38. Word before bull or stop
39. Grasshopper's rebuker
40. Baseball's DiMaggio
42. Mexican snacks
43. Isn't miserly
44. Cosmo, e.g.
45. Reverberations
46. At what time?
47. Wedding acquisition
48. Flora and fauna
49. Let up
52. Type of wine
53. Kitty starter
55. Kind of estate
56. Therefore
57. Major rug exporter
58. Unit of force
61. Rep. foe

by Raymond Hamel

ACROSS

1. Room between rooms
5. Handouts
9. Farm building
13. Opera solos
15. West Virginia resource
16. Sack starter
17. 1970 Tommy Roe hit
20. Spain's locale
21. Leslie Caron role
22. Hesitation sounds
23. Writer Bombeck
25. Swindle
26. Sweet treat
30. "Fiddler on the Roof" fellow
35. Literary collection
36. Weep loudly
37. Arctic, for one
38. Recurring theme
41. French denial
43. Lisboa's sister city
44. 1985 Kate Nelligan title role
45. Big shot
47. Calendar ender: Abbr.
48. Anglo's partner
49. Tentacled sea creature
52. Ostrich's cousin
54. Author Bellow
55. Lemon drink
58. Meadow bird
60. Drinkers' toasts
64. "Black Bottom Stomp" performer
67. Came down
68. Christmas centerpiece
69. The elder Judd
70. Critic Rex
71. Cruising
72. Tiff

DOWN

1. Pilgrim to Mecca
2. Pilgrim to Mecca
3. Citrus flavor
4. Emblem of victory
5. Item up the sleeve
6. Take it easy
7. Slander
8. With cunning
9. Visit Vail, perhaps
10. "Come Back, Little Sheba" playwright
11. Cowardly Lion portrayer
12. Chooses
14. Helical
18. Doorway parts
19. Perfect
24. Long, long time
26. Caan or Cagney
27. ___ Gay
28. Type of rubber
29. Superior to
31. Author Umberto
32. "Rigoletto" composer
33. Film director Peter
34. Tennyson's "___ Arden"
39. Odysseus's rescuer, in myth
40. Exquisitely
42. Guitarist Lofgren
46. Ecto or proto ending
49. Panel of 12
50. Alaskan river
51. Groups of indigenous plants
53. "I Remember Mama" mama
55. Partly open
56. Take out of print
57. Nobelist Wiesel
59. "Red Balloon" painter
61. On
62. ___ Linda, Calif.
63. Fit of anger
65. Former Ford
66. ___ & Perrins

by Robert Zimmerman

ACROSS

1. Gregory Hines specialty
4. Take for granted
10. Colorless
14. Actress Gardner
15. Stay-at-home
16. Roof overhang
17. House member: Abbr.
18. Interior decorator's hiree
20. Wields the gavel
22. Swear (to)
23. Pinker inside
24. Opponent
25. Greek geometer
27. Premolar
31. Pallid
32. Secrete
33. Poi ingredient
34. Fed. power agcy.
35. Diffidence
38. Sword's superior, in saying
39. Craving
41. Ends' partner
42. More than fat
44. Stereo components
46. 32-card card game
47. Effect a makeover
48. Napoleon's cavalry commander
49. Slow, in music
52. Bring an issue home
55. Pet rock, maybe
57. Hair application
58. Formerly
59. Mother ___
60. The 90's, e.g.
61. Goes out with regularly
62. Archeological finds
63. Director Howard

DOWN

1. Canvas cover
2. Declare positively
3. Houseman TV series, with "The"
4. Two are often prescribed
5. Under the elms
6. "Great!"
7. Salt Lake City team
8. Russian for "peace"
9. Makes more valuable
10. Person who's feeling down in the mouth?
11. Fad
12. Lexington and Madison: Abbr.
13. Lahr or Parks
19. One of the Aleutians
21. Shopper's lure
24. Adjutants
25. Noblemen
26. Exhaust
27. Ties
28. Toothless threat
29. "___ my case"
30. Gift recipient
32. Kind of power
36. Barn dances
37. Legendary hemlock drinker
40. Sidewinder lock-ons
43. False god
45. Actor Dullea
46. A form of 46-Across
48. Tycoon
49. Primates
50. Madonna's "Truth or ___"
51. Church area
52. Lo-cal
53. Mr. Mostel
54. Flair
56. Chow down

1	2	3	■	4	5	6	7	8	9	■	10	11	12	13
14			■	15						■	16			
17			■	18						19				
20			21					■	22					
■	■	23					■	24				■	■	■
25	26					■	27					28	29	30
31					■	32				■	33			
34			■	35	36					37	■	38		
39			40	■	41				■	42	43			
44				45				■	46					
■	■	■	47				■	48					■	■
49	50	51				■	52						53	54
55						56					■	57		
58				■	59						■	60		
61				■	62						■	63		

by John Greenman

ACROSS

1. Fitzgerald's forte
5. Shortening
9. "___ little piggy . . ."
13. Impetuous
14. Sunburn remedy
15. Rule the ___
16. Agitate
17. Have on
18. Simone's school
19. Epithet for a TV set
22. Jeanne or Thérèse: Abbr.
23. Believer in God
24. Podunk
30. Eucharistic plate
31. Lascivious looks
32. Set-to
35. On ___ with (equal to)
36. High in pitch
37. Mongol monk
38. Bandman Brown
39. Baseball's Doubleday
41. Bank patron
42. Fixation
44. "Queenie" author Michael
46. Get a move on
47. Gambler's tormentor
53. Beau ___
54. Flub
55. Eye layer
57. Take back to the car pound
58. Axlike tool
59. 60's vocalist Vikki
60. German river
61. "Let's Make a Deal" choice
62. Make a cable stitch

DOWN

1. Last year's jrs.
2. Marcus Porcius
3. M ___ Mary
4. Farm machine
5. Maker of cases
6. Not aweather
7. Abbey or Tobacco, e.g.
8. Suffix for 41-Down
9. Alarm bell
10. Catcalls
11. Wee atoll
12. Ending for hip or hoop
15. Extends a subscription
20. School founded in 1440
21. Fragrance
24. October birthstone
25. Place for a necklace clasp
26. Hellenic H's
27. Obliqueness
28. Moray pursuer
29. Aquarium fish
32. Sitarist Shankar
33. Bodement
34. Voting district
37. Politician with a limited future
39. Hurricane of 1992
40. Smile broadly
41. Word before deep or dive
42. Demosthenes e.g.
43. Impatient one
44. Bumped impolitely
45. Spanish direction
47. Grimm villain
48. "Yipes!"
49. Old fogy
50. Dolt
51. Netman Lendl
52. Garr of "Tootsie"
56. Trump's "The ___ of the Deal"

by Bette Sue Cohen

ACROSS

1. Bend
5. Exchange
9. Polite form of address
13. Actor Calhoun
14. Make ___ for (argue in support of)
15. Ray of Hollywood
16. This puzzle's mystery subject
19. "The Joy Luck Club" author
20. Fuzzy
21. Rule
22. Yield
23. Dubbed one
24. 1951 movie with 16-Across
31. Stumble
32. River to the Caspian
33. Veterans Day mo.
35. Daly of "Gypsy"
36. Competition for Geraldo
38. Trig function
39. Wynken, Blynken and ___
40. They're sometimes wild
41. Earth mover
42. 1957 movie with 16-Across
47. Thumbnail sketch
48. 16-Across's "Cat on ___ Tin Roof"
49. Étagère piece
52. County north of San Francisco
54. Neighbor of Ind.
57. 1946 movie with 16-Across
60. "___ known then what . . ."
61. Cancel
62. "A" code word
63. Greek portico
64. Use épées
65. Half a fortnight

DOWN

1. Stew
2. "Damn Yankees" seductress
3. Green land
4. ___ Affair
5. Play's start
6. He coined the term "horsepower"
7. Pallid
8. Caress
9. M-G-M's Louis B. and others
10. "___ know is what . . ."
11. Sick as ___
12. Dawn
14. Put up with
17. Novelist Waugh
18. Disney mermaid
22. Horn, for one
23. Iranian chief, once
24. Letter abbr.
25. Richard of "Bustin' Loose"
26. Newswoman Ellerbee
27. Tend to
28. Refrain syllable
29. Confederacy's opponent
30. Three trios
34. Exceedingly
36. Eight: Prefix
37. Through
38. Latched
40. Law professor Hill
43. Airline to Spain
44. Outpouring of gossip
45. Bit of fall weather
46. Miss O'Neill
49. Publisher Adolph
50. Sloop
51. Defense means
52. Diner's guide
53. First-class
54. Man or Ely, e.g.
55. 16-Across's "___ With Father"
56. Plumber's concern
58. Travel (about)
59. 16-Across's "The Last Time I ___ Paris"

by Wayne Robert Williams

ACROSS

1. Interlaced
6. Canadian tree
11. Unit of chewing tobacco
14. Idiotic
15. Relieve
16. One of Frank's exes
17. Motion picture award
19. ___ Kippur
20. ___ ex machina
21. Red Square figure
23. Spacecraft sections
27. Tentative forays
29. Gone from the program
30. Shoulders-to-hips areas
31. "___ Irish Rose"
32. Paper purchases
33. Once existed
36. Guitarist Lofgren
37. See 30-Down
38. ___ fide
39. Farm enclosure
40. Crude characters
41. Gershwin hero
42. Jai alai ball
44. "Ode to ___ Joe"
45. Votes
47. Hamlet, at times
48. Shrine to remember
49. Spotted
50. Reunion-goers
51. Nature personified
58. First lady
59. "Middlemarch" author
60. Inventor Howe
61. Matched grouping
62. Tears
63. Show shock, e.g.

DOWN

1. Store-bought hair
2. Musician Yoko
3. Actor Kilmer
4. Football lineman
5. Tries to rile
6. John Fowles novel, with "The"
7. "___ Well That Ends Well"
8. Hebron grp.
9. Big, friendly dog, for short
10. Huxley's "___ in Gaza"
11. Teen film hit of 1992
12. To have, to Héloise
13. Curses
18. Require
22. "Xanadu" musical grp.
23. Signifies
24. Pluto's path
25. Perry's paper
26. Functions
27. Bubble masses
28. Columnist Bombeck
30. With 37-Across, the ground
32. Wild times
34. 1973 Rolling Stones hit
35. Word with nay or sooth
37. Bit of poetry
38. Manila machete
40. Early feminist
41. Avant-gardist
43. Slippery ___
44. Rabbit's title
45. Hardens, as clay
46. Breathing
47. Borscht Ingredients
49. Bullet-riddled
52. Cheer
53. Malleable metal
54. Pale or Newcastle brown
55. Narrow inlet
56. Middle X or O
57. Presidential initials

by Joel Davajan

ACROSS

1. Unhappy
5. Man with the world on his shoulders
10. Israeli carrier
14. "Mona ___"
15. Scarlett's love
16. Comic Rudner
17. What we celebrate on July 4
20. Honor, with "to"
21. Form 1040 amount
22. Buntline and Rorem
23. Sean Connery, e.g.
24. Duke's home
27. Fifth Avenue name
28. Catch in the act
31. Gaucho's rope
32. Golfer Ballesteros
33. Old Russian assembly
34. What we observe on July 4
37. Bronze and Iron
38. Some intersections
39. Think
40. Stag party attendees
41. Scorch
42. Ranch
43. Tools locale
44. ___ de foie gras
45. Book after Nehemiah
48. Fortification
52. What we watch on July 4
54. A lulu
55. Miss Brooks portrayer
56. Muck
57. Witnessed
58. Stocking material
59. Some whiskies

DOWN

1. Happy
2. Green shade
3. Employed
4. Seasons, as meat
5. Teen hangout
6. Dean Martin's "___ Amore"
7. ___ majesté
8. Arm of the Treasury Dept.
9. Ill
10. Construct
11. Island near Venice
12. Mighty mite
13. Costly cloth
18. Hangover soother?
19. Son of Seth
23. Baseball and hockey stats
24. Father of Hector and Paris
25. Danny of the N.B.A.
26. Weighed down
27. Passover feast
28. Blue entertainment
29. Hotpoint rival
30. Sang to the moon
32. Golf legend Sam
33. Doctor's instrument
35. Intangible
36. Egypt's Church
41. "Good night, ___" (old TV phrase)
42. Briny
43. Like Samson, once
44. Kind of truck
45. Heroic poetry
46. "Auld Lang ___"
47. It's better known for its bark than its bite
48. Third degrees, usually
49. Seaman's shout
50. Nod off
51. Rams' dams
53. Dernier ___

by Sidney L. Robbins

ACROSS

1. High rung on the evolutionary ladder
6. Alternative to a shower
10. Quatrain rhyme scheme
14. Like ___ from the blue
15. Environs
16. Wise guy
17. Popular chocolate snack
19. On the level
20. River through Florence
21. Mother ___
22. Help in crime
23. Quad number
24. Lock
25. Torah readers
29. Forgiving one
32. Oscar, e.g.
33. Prefix with cycle
34. Draft org.
37. March events?
40. Lolita
42. Phony prefix
43. Fond du ___, Wis
44. New Zealand native
45. Where Spain and Portugal are
48. Seasoning
49. Afterward
51. Kind of show
53. Singer Minnelli
54. Kick locale
56. Dumb ___
60. Paid promotion: Abbr.
61. Give up hard drink?
63. Vegetarian's no-no
64. Sheltered
65. Similar
66. Wan
67. Lease
68. Little ones

DOWN

1. It's a laugh
2. "Deutschland ___ Alles"
3. Daybreak
4. What's more
5. To the ___ degree
6. Louisiana waterway
7. Bowers
8. Socials
9. Tortoise's competitor
10. Glaring
11. Place to have one's head examined
12. Bouts of chills
13. Borscht ingredients
18. Selves
23. Hoedown musician
24. Shortened
25. Criticizes
26. Not at home
27. Coming-of-age event
28. Cross-one's-heart garment
30. Play on words
31. Some
35. Dried
36. Agitate
38. Unit of corn
39. Phys. or chem.
41. Baby food
46. "Reds" star
47. Out of bed
48. Bygone
49. Andean animal
50. Gofers
52. Commencement
54. Box lightly
55. Patriot Nathan
56. It's full of baloney
57. Final notice
58. Roué
59. War deity
62. Hardly an underperformer

by Wayne Robert Williams

ACROSS

1. Comic Martha
5. Bamboozle
9. Stoppers
14. Height: Abbr.
15. Face-to-face exam
16. Beau at the balcony
17. Town near Caen
18. Chockablock
20. Headlong
22. Resident's suffix
23. Race tracks
24. Dormitory din
28. Radio transmission sites
30. Offspring, genealogically: Abbr.
31. Celtic Neptune
32. Centers
33. Walk-on
34. Chancellorsville victor
35. Western Indian
36. Enmity
38. Sugar suffix
39. Singer Tillis
40. Word after many or honey
41. Conflict in Greek drama
42. French dance
43. A.L. or N.L. honorees
44. "Phèdre" dramatist
46. Flummoxes
48. Spring fragrance
49. Picture blowup: Abbr.
50. Head count
53. Game of digs and spikes
57. Parts of pelvises
58. Greek poet saved by a dolphin
59. Fit
60. Oodles
61. Mississippi Senator ___ Lott
62. Branch headquarters?
63. "Auld Lang ___"

DOWN

1. Answer: Abbr.
2. Der ___ (Adenauer moniker)
3. Cowardly one
4. Changes with the times
5. Carpentry pins
6. Europe/Asia separator
7. Dark shadow
8. Building wing
9. 1984 Goldie Hawn movie
10. Look threatening
11. Actress Thurman
12. Solidify
13. Our sun
19. Xmas tree trimming
21. Spoil
24. Interstate trucks
25. Without rhyme or reason
26. "Schindler's List" star Liam
27. Novelist Graham
28. Hitches, as a ride
29. Surpass at the dinner table
30. Natural alarm clocks
33. Hoofbeats
36. About to occur
37. Pulchritudinous
41. Gum arabic trees
44. Garden brook
45. Completely
47. Juicy fruit
48. Takes it easy
50. Contemporary dramatist David
51. King of the beasts
52. Deceased
53. Large tub
54. Hockey's Bobby
55. Golf-ball position
56. Prohibit

36

by Albert J. Klaus

ACROSS

1. "Woe is me!"
5. Inn, informally
10. Dollop
14. Frolic
15. Title holder
16. Burt's ex
17. Jai ___
18. Former auto executive
20. Two-pointers
22. Differs
23. Saucer occupants for short
24. Mozart's "___ fan tutte"
25. Ball girl
28. Vacation spot
30. "Jerusalem Delivered" poet
34. Border lake
35. Car in a procession
37. Spring mo.
38. West Point salutatorian, 1829
41. Language ending
42. Off course
43. City two hours south of Lillehammer
44. Spreads the word
46. Bit of voodoo
47. Grueling tests
48. Sword with a guard
50. Louis Freeh's org.
51. Rubbed
54. Ascendant
58. Two-time U.S. Open golf champion
61. Kind of shark
62. Suffix with buck
63. Pentax rival
64. Sicilian rumbler
65. Poet Robert ___ Warren
66. Exhausted
67. Sunup direction

DOWN

1. Bedouin
2. She gets what she wants
3. Amo, ___, amat
4. Modern film maker
5. Leaves in a hurry
6. Wows
7. Jet's heading
8. Mercury and Jupiter, e.g.
9. "Well done!"
10. Actress DeHaven
11. Places
12. ___ over lightly
13. Kind of crime
19. Mobile unit?
21. Season of l'année
24. Polish producer
25. Cap
26. Having an irregular edge
27. Defame
28. Boil
29. Military chaplain
31. Hot sauce
32. Word with cold or breathing
33. Chocolate snacks
35. Elevations: Abbr.
36. Remark
39. Hardly one with a lilting voice
40. Neoprimitive American artist
45. Unextinguished
47. Kimono sash
49. Paradises
50. Weather line
51. Keep time manually
52. "You are ___"
53. Ages and ages
54. Soon
55. Ninth Greek letter
56. Actress Woods and others
57. Pest
59. One who gets special treatment
60. W.W. II hero

1	2	3	4	■	5	6	7	8	9	■	10	11	12	13
14				■	15					■	16			
17				■	18					19				
20				21			■	■	22					
■	■	■	23			■	■	24				■	■	■
25	26	27			■	28	29		■	30		31	32	33
34				■	35				36		■	37		
38				39							40			
41			■	42						■	43			
44			45		■	46			■	47				
■	■	■	48		49		■	■	50			■	■	■
51	52	53				■	■	54				55	56	57
58						59	60			■	61			
62				■	63					■	64			
65				■	66					■	67			

by Thomas W. Schier

ACROSS

1. Say "I do" again
6. March starter
9. Diplomatic skills
14. Dwelling place
15. U.N. member
16. Honolulu hello
17. Scrabble, anagrams, etc.
19. Bottoms of graphs
20. Disney dog
21. House of Lords members
22. Mosque chiefs
23. Ave. crossers
24. "I've been ___!"
25. City on the Brazos
27. Ear cleaner
29. ___ race (finished first)
30. Lived
33. Oaxaca waters
35. Dictionaries and thesauruses
37. Organic soil
38. Subject of this puzzle
39. Lockup
40. Preambles
42. "You ___ Have to Be So Nice"
43. "The Sultan of Sulu" author
44. Crooner Williams
45. Jokester's props
46. Nightclub bits
47. Tricia Nixon ___
48. New Deal org.
51. Move furtively
54. Barely open
56. Bewail
57. Start of the French workweek
58. Some of them are famous
60. Not ___ in the world
61. Prayer word
62. ___ nous
63. Ex-baseball commish Ueberroth
64. Light time
65. Lucy's landlady

DOWN

1. Singer Lou
2. Enemy vessel
3. T H I S
H E R E
I R O N
S E N T
4. Whirlpool
5. B.A. or Ph.D.
6. Like August weather, perhaps
7. Client
8. Computer access codes
9. City vehicle
10. Battle depicted in "The Last Command"
11. Hip joint
12. Not us
13. Freshness
18. Quickly: Abbr.
24. Towel word
26. Connectors
28. Housebroken
29. Circumlocutory
30. Poet laureate, 1843–50
31. Similar
32. Mil. officer
33. ___ Romeo
34. Well-mannered
35. Incoherent speech
36. Off Broadway award
38. Is obstinate
41. More erratic
42. Humanitarian Dorothea
45. Where a cruise calls
46. Previn or Kostelanetz
47. Disk jockey Kasem
49. San Diego pro
50. Photographer Adams
51. Masher's comeuppance
52. Politico Clare Boothe ___
53. ___ the finish
55. Al Hirt hit
56. ___ Blanc
59. Itsy-bitsy

38

by Sidney L. Robbins

ACROSS

1. Brazilian dance
6. Teen woe
10. Loot
14. "The Tempest" sprite
15. Avoid
16. Sherwood Anderson's "Winesburg, ___"
17. Letter turner
19. Home for some crocodiles
20. Crimson foes
21. Ones who brood
22. Sees socially
23. Artist Magritte
24. Measured (out)
25. Sir Isaac
29. Teeter
31. Singer Merman
32. Beauty's companion
33. Oklahoma city
36. Comedian Jerry
38. Neck artery
40. Tit for ___
41. Destroy for fun
43. Tip over
44. Storied Plaza girl
46. Alarms
47. Square: e.g.
48. Help in mischief
50. Makes a mess
51. Off base, maybe
52. Use a letter opener
56. Papal name
57. "Perils of Pauline" star
59. Otherwise
60. First name in mysteries
61. Movado rival
62. Not natural
63. Olympian's quest
64. You'll get a rise out of this

DOWN

1. Pack rat's motto
2. Asia's ___ Sea
3. 60's fashion
4. Writer Hecht and others
5. Pie ___ mode
6. Wan
7. One-fifth of humankind
8. Goofy
9. Opposite WSW
10. "Moonlight," e.g.
11. Arkansas location
12. Felt below par
13. "Here ___!"
18. Invitation info
22. Ruin
23. Stylish desks
24. Tableland
25. Egg container
26. Ms. Kett of old comics
27. Executive branch
28. Part of ITT: Abbr.
30. Per
32. Women's support group?
34. Eat well
35. Puts two and two together
37. Admiral Perry victory site
39. W.W. II agcy.
42. Beach protector
45. Like an unpaid policy
46. Wall Street order
47. In a foxy way
49. Yawning?
50. Raced
51. Space prefix
52. Tree locale
53. Valentino co-star ___ Lee
54. Residents: Suffix
55. Not pictures
57. "___ o' My Heart"
58. Kind of humor

1	2	3	4	5	■	6	7	8	9	■	10	11	12	13
14					■	15				■	16			
17					18					■	19			
20				■	21				■	22				
■	■	■	■	23				■	24					■
25	26	27	28			■	29	30					■	■
31					■	32					■	33	34	35
36					37		■	38			39			
40			■	41			42		■	43				
■	■	44	45					■	46					
■	47					■	48	49			■	■	■	■
50					■	51				■	52	53	54	55
56				■	57					58				
59				■	60				■	61				
62				■	63				■	64				

by Lois Sidway

ACROSS

1. Mississippi Senator Cochran
5. Nutty
9. Gangbusters at the box office
14. River to the Rhine
15. Lena of recent films
16. Like the skies in "Ulalume"
17. Sorts
18. Carty of baseball
19. Oh, so many moons
20. Go astray
23. Stack-blowing feeling
24. Countdown start
25. Tak's opposite
26. Alphabetical run
27. As a whole
31. Bit
33. Mezzo-soprano Marilyn
34. Santa Fe Trail town
35. Pickle
38. Red of firefighting fame
39. Words of wonderment
40. With respect to
41. "Whip It" rock group
42. Drawing card
43. The Divine Miss M.
44. Play the siren
46. Smelt, e.g.
47. Aquarium oddity
49. Cry of delight
50. It has its point
51. Harvest goddess
52. Not yet in full bloom
58. Tubby the Tuba creator Paul
60. Reed of note
61. Light-footed
62. Hint
63. An order of the court
64. W.W. I German admiral
65. Pond covering
66. Silent O.K.'s
67. With defects and all

DOWN

1. Shadow
2. Christmas play prop
3. Synagogue cabinets
4. Not dose
5. World's third-largest island
6. '79 sci-fi thriller
7. Muscle spasms
8. Bird that summers in the Arctic
9. Agree
10. Sugary suffix
11. Many skiers use these when they [see diagonal]
12. Writers Jean and Walter
13. Assault
21. Mink's relative
22. Pretension
27. '64 musical "___ a Ball"
28. Leaf's starting point
29. Getting across
30. Stew ingredient
31. Skier Phil
32. Original Jed Clampett
34. Score for Barry Sanders
36. Observe
37. Great Scott of 1857
40. Sound as ___
42. Animal that sleeps with its eyes open
45. Noodle topper
46. Candy
47. Must, slangily
48. Part of an Argentine autumn
50. Steer clear of
53. River of Spain
54. Greek peak
55. Third addendum to a letter
56. ". . . ___ saw Elba"
57. Shoemakers' bottles
59. Trevino's org.

by Joel Davajan

ACROSS

1. Rolling stone's deficiency
5. Anchor position
10. Complain
14. Aleutian island
15. ___ Loa
16. Literally "high wood"
17. Obstinate
20. Royal spouses
21. Be on the brink
22. Professional bean counters
23. Designer Christian
24. Hardy's pal
27. Describe
28. Org. founded in 1948
31. Bandleader Shaw
32. Imparted
33. Sondheim's "___ the Woods"
34. Elusive
37. Branch Davidians, e.g.
38. Speaker's platform
39. Worker's wish
40. Off ___ tangent
41. Curb, with "in"
42. Daredevil acts
43. Actor Sean
44. Lady in an apron
45. "Yessir," e.g.
48. Moon of Jupiter
52. In the altogether
54. Final notice
55. Teach one-on-one
56. Lion's den
57. Like 52-Across
58. Atlanta university
59. Thompson of "Howards End"

DOWN

1. Opposite of fem.
2. Mr. Preminger
3. Daze
4. Like the 2 in B_2
5. Not knowing right from wrong
6. Small pies
7. Hosiery snags
8. Actress Claire
9. Diversions
10. Future star
11. Border on
12. Actor's part
13. Look with squinty eyes
18. Sheepish lass
19. A long time
23. Prima donnas
24. Rope a dogie
25. Senator Specter
26. City east of Syracuse
27. Store up
28. ___ a million
29. Alamogordo event, 7/16/45
30. Shoe bottoms
32. Rye or corn
33. Silent, or almost so
35. Toothless
36. With pretentiousness
41. Tear
42. Compensation
43. Pro golfer Calvin
44. TV's "___ Dad"
45. Presently
46. "Elephant Boy" star, 1937
47. Have brake problems
48. Roman statesman and censor
49. Thailand, once
50. Adjust the sails
51. Polish border river
53. Add

1	2	3	4	■	5	6	7	8	9	■	10	11	12	13
14				■	15					■	16			
17				18						19				
20								■	21					
■	■	■	22				■	23				■	■	■
24	25	26				■	27				■	28	29	30
31					■	32				■	33			
34					35					36				
37				■	38				■	39				
40			■	41				■	42					
■	■	■	43				■	44				■	■	■
45	46	47				■	48					49	50	51
52						53								
54				■	55					■	56			
57				■	58					■	59			

by Eric Albert

ACROSS

1. Colorful salad ingredient
10. Plant pest
15. Throw some light on
16. El ___ (Spanish painter)
17. Acting ambassador
19. Mooring rope
20. The sky, maybe
21. Perry's creator
22. Pop's Carly or Paul
25. It's a drag
27. Country rtes.
28. It has its ups and downs
30. Turner of Hollywood
31. "Duke Bluebeard's Castle" composer
32. Super-soaked
33. Literature as art
36. Urger's words
37. Aloha State
38. Ooze
39. Bombast
40. 70's sitcom "___ Sharkey"
43. Watered-down ideas
44. Subsequently
45. Teri of "Tootsie"
46. "___ Andronicus"
48. Samantha's "Bewitched" husband
50. Facetious advice in a mystery
54. Indoor design
55. Carouse
56. Birthplace of 16-Across
57. By and large

DOWN

1. ". . . for ___ for poorer"
2. Founder of est
3. Talks Dixie-style
4. Diagram a sentence
5. Competitive advantage
6. Boat's departure site
7. Rocket's departure site
8. It's after zeta
9. Foul caller
10. One more time
11. Schoolmarmish
12. Birthright
13. Bar accessory
14. ___ Passos
18. Go with the ___
22. Layup alternative
23. Quarantine
24. Be militaristic
26. Manner
28. It can sting
29. Before, in palindromes
30. Actress ___ Singer
31. Radar screen image
32. Rouse to action
33. Brief break
34. It's worth looking into
35. Clavell's "___ Pan"
36. Recipe abbr.
39. Mess-hall meal
40. Clint Eastwood's city
41. Kind of scream
42. Obstinate
44. Pelf
45. Miss Garbo
47. Jog
48. Hamlet, for one
49. Nowhere near
50. Fed. medical detectives
51. Sunny-side-up item
52. Lawyer Baird
53. Cambodia's ___ Nol

by Joel Davajan

ACROSS

1. Christiania today
5. Noggin tops
10. Hind's mate
14. Hullabaloo
15. Open-eyed
16. "Damn Yankees" vamp
17. Ike was one
20. Track officials
21. Testify
22. "Rule, Britannia" composer
23. Early Briton
24. Social groups
27. Garlic relative
28. Asian holiday
31. Culture mores
32. Coxswain's crew
33. ___ Marquette
34. G.I. newspaper
37. Cures leather
38. "That's interesting"
39. Opt
40. Two-by-two vessel
41. Reared
42. Worth
43. Shed
44. Escape
45. Roman villa locale
48. Apollyon adherent
52. Biblical beacon
54. Seller's caveat
55. Backcomb hair
56. Mechanical memorization
57. Smoker's sound
58. Mead research site
59. Animal team

DOWN

1. Switch settings
2. Eye opening
3. Kind of flow
4. Bell workers
5. Thin metal disks
6. Cognizant
7. Salts
8. Dr.'s graph
9. Most rundown
10. Nodded
11. Pamplona runner
12. Hale of "Gilligan's Island"
13. 10 on the Beaufort scale
18. Pressure
19. Spoon
23. Intrinsically
24. Jai alai basket
25. It makes scents
26. Part of the evening
27. Put on cargo
28. Dakota digs
29. Upright
30. Blood and acid, e.g.
32. Beginning
33. Bohemian beers
35. Berlin events of 1948
36. Recap
41. Machetelike knife
42. Wimbledon champ Gibson
43. Code name
44. 1980 DeLuise flick
45. Royal Russian
46. "___ girl!"
47. Ski spot
48. Coal stratum
49. Hotcakes acronym
50. Bristle
51. Revenuers, for short
53. "___ sport"

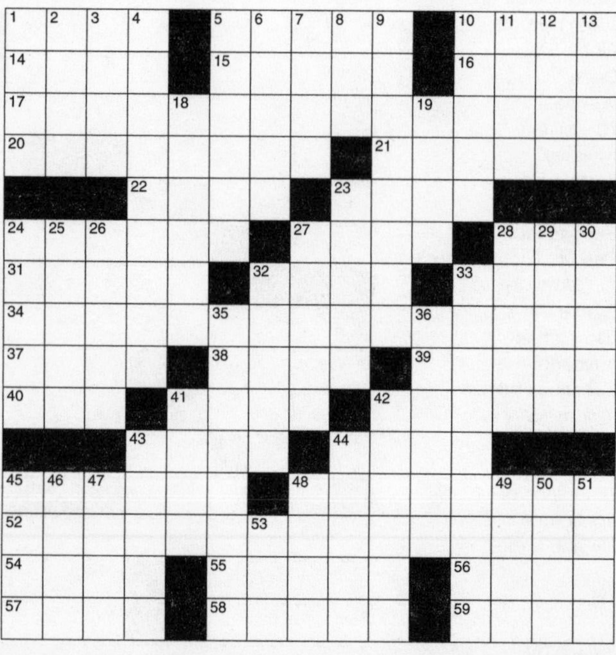

by Janie Lyons

ACROSS

1. Dog star
5. Gull's cousin
9. Eyeball bender
14. Ground grain
15. Mini revelation
16. Red-eyed bird
17. Haitian despot
20. Cordwood measure
21. Dance in a shtetl
22. Out's opposite
23. Vidal's Breckinridge
25. Actor Young of TV's 67-Across
27. Is grief-stricken
30. Book subtitled "His Songs and His Sayings"
35. Supped
36. Relative of a Bap. or Presb.
37. Balkan capital
38. Gabor sister
40. Thimbleful
42. Dryden work
43. Help get situated
45. Plugs of a sort
47. Saturn's wife
48. 1956 Rosalind Russell role
50. "For ___ us a child is born"
51. Headlight?
52. Survey chart
54. Seaweed product
57. ___ fixe
59. Reached the total of
63. Popular psychologist
66. Paul Anka hit
67. See 25-Across
68. Deep blue
69. Throat malady
70. Achy
71. James Mason sci-fi role of 1954

DOWN

1. Rock band equipment
2. Usher
3. Mend, in a way
4. Alternatives to The Club
5. Round stopper
6. Delights
7. Change the décor
8. Kind of network
9. Roman breakfast?
10. Light beers
11. "Jewel Song," e.g.
12. Mariner's peril
13. Raced
18. She played Grace Van Owen on "L.A. Law"
19. Passepartout, to Phileas Fogg
24. Strongly scented plant
26. Stellar Ram
27. Fiji neighbor
28. City in northern Japan
29. Set in motion
31. Dinnerware
32. Building contractor
33. Not suitable
34. Final authority
36. Madness
39. Oust
41. Nurse, maybe
44. Directed toward a goal
46. Hair fixative
49. Office connections?
50. Donny Osmond, e.g.
53. Record-holding N.F.L. receiver ___ Monk
54. Postfixes
55. Sandpaper surface
56. Opened a crack
58. Catalonian river
60. Hawaiian hen
61. In shape
62. "Kon-Tiki" Museum site
64. Shrill bark
65. Lyric poem

by Ronald C. Hirschfeld

ACROSS

1. They're plucked
6. Busy as ___
10. Lake formed by Hoover Dam
14. Bye
15. Druid, e.g.
16. Presque ___, Me.
17. Close behind
20. Chair plan
21. Setter or retriever
22. "Fables in Slang" author
24. Part of a bridal bio
25. Words after "The last time I saw Paris"
34. Buck follower
35. Muddies the water
36. "The Company"
37. Bara and Negri
39. Years in Paris
40. Mole
42. Native: Suffix
43. Comedienne Fields
45. Hebrides language
46. Completely unperturbed
50. Olympian: Abbr.
51. Knock-knock joke, e.g.
52. Sounds the hour
56. 1967–70 war site
61. Discourage
63. Japanese aboriginal
64. Assassinate
65. Put up
66. Cuff
67. Cod relative
68. Drinks with straws

DOWN

1. It's a laugh
2. 1985 film "My Life as ___"
3. ___ of passage
4. Drudge
5. Dairy bar order
6. Otto's "oh!"
7. English channel, with "the"
8. Like many textbook publishers
9. Adjective for Rome
10. Cellar growth
11. Old gas brand
12. Sleep like ___
13. Excellent, in slang
18. Cry of achievement
19. Ancient capital of Macedonian kings
23. Corrigenda
25. June in Hollywood
26. Sister of Thalia
27. Alfa ___
28. Sock ___
29. Quinine water
30. Smarten
31. Lip-puckering
32. Hair-coloring solution
33. ___ et Magistra (1961 encyclical)
38. It causes sparks
41. Lapidarist's object of study
44. City on Lake Winnebago
47. Tar
48. Actor Gooding
49. Glues
52. Earth
53. Bluefin
54. Scat cat
55. It's north of Neb.
57. Flying: Prefix
58. TV exec Friendly
59. Cape ___ (westernmost point in continental Europe)
60. Colonists
61. ___ de deux
62. Fork

by David A. Rosen

ACROSS

1. Rumble
6. Not fancy?
10. Difficult obligation
14. "___ of do or die"
15. Bing Crosby best seller
16. Guthrie the younger
17. Hearty entree
20. Kibbutzniks' dance
21. Reverse
22. Must
23. Place to crash
25. Kipling novel
26. Tasty side dish
35. Mortgage matter
36. Words before "in the arm" or "in the dark"
37. Detective's cry
38. Them in "Them!"
39. Common key signature
40. Composer ___ Carlo Menotti
41. Cpl., for one
42. Feed a fete
43. Stood for
44. Yummy dessert
47. Cherbourg chum
48. Latin I?
49. Lamb Chop's "spokesperson"
52. Oceania republic
55. Windmill segment
59. Eventual bonus?
62. Cream-filled sandwich
63. Debouchment
64. Internet patrons
65. Blubber
66. Yeltsin veto
67. Koch's predecessor

DOWN

1. Calculator work
2. Radar blip
3. Thieves' hideout
4. They're loose
5. "Yikes!"
6. "The Afternoon of a ___"
7. In the thick of
8. First name in perfumery
9. Venture
10. Japanese mat
11. Olympic hawk
12. Bed-frame crosspiece
13. "Mikado" executioner
18. Sport whose name means "soft way"
19. Polo, e.g.
24. Circulars
25. Carpenter's woe
26. Old French bread?
27. High-priced spread?
28. ". . . and eat ___"
29. Subj. of a Clinton victory, 11/17/93
30. Key
31. Midway alternative
32. River nymph
33. The Gold Coast, today
34. "A votre ___!"
39. Java neighbor
40. Columbus, by birth
42. "Nancy" or "Cathy"
43. Puss
45. Server on skates
46. Dos + cuatro
49. Take third
50. Take on
51. "___ on Film" (1983 book set)
52. Conniving
53. Coach Nastase
54. Rock's Joan
56. Sphere
57. "Cheers" habitué
58. Alternatively
60. Lady lobster
61. Ungainly craft

by Albert J. Klaus

ACROSS

1. John Denver's "Christmas in ___"
6. "Tuna-Fishing" painter
10. Among
14. "___ Eyes" (1969 song)
15. Actor Richard
16. Bounty rival
17. Refinement
18. Witticisms
19. Vigor
20. 1950 Sinatra hit
23. West Bank org.
24. "Just a ___"
25. Three strokes, perhaps
28. Actress Sommer
31. Shares
36. Feared test
38. Troubles
40. Weaken
41. 1955 Sinatra hit
44. Improve
45. Rig
46. Shut off
47. Beachwear
49. Relax
51. Audit conductor, for short
52. Guy's date
54. Eternity
56. 1961 Sinatra hit
64. "Warm"
65. Minnow eater
66. Driving hazard
68. Petruchio's mate
69. Shillelagh land
70. 10th-day-of-Christmas gift
71. Swerve
72. Henna and others
73. Follow

DOWN

1. Blue-chip symbol
2. Lively dance
3. Chihuahua change
4. Bar, in law
5. Compass part
6. Half begun?
7. Excited
8. Stucco backing
9. Foot part
10. Swear
11. Ryun's run
12. Basil's successor
13. Niels Bohr, e.g.
21. The Man Without a Country
22. More aloof
25. Propels a gondola
26. Bouquet
27. Bird "perched upon a bust of Pallas"
29. Toddlers
30. Dramatist Rice
32. Goddess of discord
33. Raccoon kin
34. Lawn tool
35. Is apparent
37. Impart
39. Ditto
42. Saw
43. Elevated
48. Stood up
50. Kind of switch
53. Distrustful
55. Run site
56. Prepares the presses
57. Plumber's concern
58. Behind
59. Ale
60. Pennsylvania port
61. Roadhouses
62. They go into locks
63. Relative of Hindustani
67. Volte-face WNW

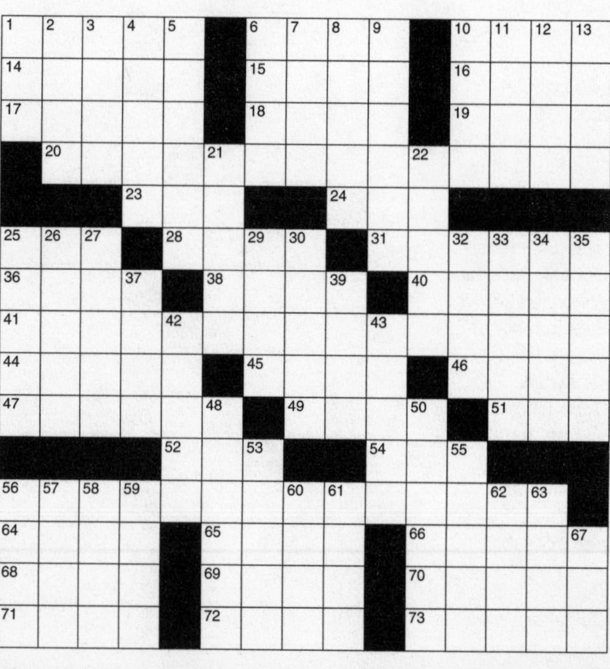

ACROSS

1. Crocus bulb
5. "Son of the Sun"
9. Set to
14. Pastiche
15. Score in pinochle
16. "A house is not ___"
17. Restaurant request
18. Vessel for Jill
19. "Anticipation" singer
20. Song by 11-Down
23. Vinegary
24. Scottish hillside
25. Westernmost Aleutian
27. A clef
32. Unsettle?
35. Scruff
38. "Aeneid" locale
39. Musical or song by 11-Down
42. Writer Wiesel
43. Rows before P
44. Gorky's "The ___ Depths"
45. Had a hunch
47. Carol
49. Daffy Duck talk
52. Bedtime annoyances
56. Song by 11-Down
61. Mercutio's friend
62. Cigar's end
63. Prefix with China
64. An acid
65. Alert
66. Ending with gang or mob
67. Guided a raft
68. Kane's Rosebud
69. Libel, e.g.

DOWN

1. Pause sign
2. Relating to $C_{18}H_{34}O_2$
3. Dyeing instruction
4. Some handlebars
5. Collision
6. Circa
7. Mountaineer
8. Psychiatrist Alfred
9. Former Tennessee Senator Jim
10. I.O.U.
11. Late, great composer
12. Mine: Fr
13. "State of Grace" star
21. Thurber's Walter
22. Informal goodbye
26. Word on a coin
28. Student of animal behavior
29. Make Coffee
30. Knowledge
31. Spectator
32. Farm mothers
33. Base
34. "The doctor ___"
36. Barley beard
37. Exploited worker
40. It may be golden
41. Actress Verdugo
46. Friend of Harvey the rabbit
48. Belgian port
50. Mergansers kin
51. Perfumery bit
53. Showed allegiance in a way
54. Downy bird
55. Stable sound
56. Envelop
57. Our genus
58. Biographer Ludwig
59. Hawaiian honker
60. To be, to Henri

1	2	3	4	■	5	6	7	8	■	9	10	11	12	13
14				■	15				■	16				
17				■	18				■	19				
20				21					22					
23						■	24				■	■	■	■
■	■	■	25			26	■	■	27		28	29	30	31
32	33	34			■	35	36	37		■	38			
39					40					41				
42				■	43				■	44				
45				46		■	■	47	48			■	■	■
■	■	■	■	49		50	51	■	52			53	54	55
56	57	58	59					60						
61					■	62				■	63			
64					■	65				■	66			
67					■	68				■	69			

by Joel Davajan

ACROSS

1. College digs
5. Haggadah-reading time
10. Coarse hominy
14. Piedmont city
15. Cuisine type
16. The Magi, e.g.
17. Railbird's passion
20. Certain wind
21. Check
22. Opposite of "yippee!"
23. Buyer caveat
24. Bottoms
27. Darlings
28. Railroad abbr.
31. Old toy company
32. Trim
33. It's not a dime a dozen
34. Bettor's bible
37. Grocery buy
38. Sword of sport
39. Archaic "prior"
40. Political abbr.
41. Cutting reminder?
42. Didn't quite rain
43. Broadcasts
44. Baptism, e.g.
45. Corner piece?
48. Some legal documents
52. Across-the-board bet
54. Mont. neighbor
55. Mercantilism
56. Mrs. Chaplin
57. Curaçao ingredient
58. Downy duck
59. Snoopy

DOWN

1. Desert dessert
2. Agcy. founded in 1970
3. Hwys.
4. Results of some errors
5. Summer wear
6. Some House of Lords members
7. Word before free or calls
8. Ike's command, for short
9. Double-check the seat belts
10. Muddles
11. "Judith" composer
12. Cold war fighters
13. Starting gate
18. Like some gates
19. A Kringle
23. Penthouse home?
24. Pheasant broods
25. Words to live by
26. Stoop
27. Race-track runner
28. Snob
29. Notre planète
30. 1947 Horse of the Year
32. "___ Got a Brand New Bag"
33. Track hiatus time
35. Have fun
36. Like trotters, e.g.
41. Dust collector?
42. Actor Martin
43. Dismay
44. "The Cloister and the Hearth" author
45. Switch
46. Roofing item
47. Chip in
48. Interpret
49. "Git!"
50. Geologists' times
51. Waffle
53. Derníer ___

1	2	3	4	■	5	6	7	8	9	■	10	11	12	13
14				■	15					■	16			
17				18						19				
20								■	21					
■	■	■	22				■	23				■	■	■
24	25	26				■	27				■	28	29	30
31					■	32				■	33			
34					35					36				
37				■	38				■	39				
40			■	41				■	42					
■	■	■	43				■	44				■	■	■
45	46	47				■	48					49	50	51
52						53								
54				■	55					■	56			
57				■	58					■	59			

49

by Robert Zimmerman

ACROSS

1. Rig
5. Big dos
10. At a distance
14. Ur locale
15. New York's ___ Tully Hall
16. Berg opera
17. M
20. Kicker's aid
21. Names in a Saudi phone book
22. Bury
23. Cut and run
24. Yearn
26. Talk radio guest
29. Playwright O'Casey
30. Army rank, for short
33. African lily
34. Brazzaville's river
35. Through
36. H
40. Fabergé objet
41. Collection
42. Candied items
43. 1969 Three Dog Night hit
44. Pup's complaints
45. Talent for cocktail talk
47. Some heirs
48. Time founder
49. "Orlando" author
52. Forum fashion
53. Quarry
56. Y
60. Organ setting
61. Type style
62. Eros
63. Ruptured
64. Tell's target
65. Currycomb target

DOWN

1. Investigate, in a way
2. Tribe whose name means "cat people"
3. Old gray animal?
4. Some ratings
5. Newgate guard
6. 1966 Caine role
7. Wagons ___
8. German cry
9. Bishop's domain
10. Solo
11. Candid cameraman
12. Der ___ (Adenauer)
13. Krupp family home
18. Tall writing?
19. Tiny swimmer
23. Took off
24. Director Marshall
25. "Othello" plotter
26. Item in a locket
27. Collimate
28. Moose, e.g.
29. Divans
30. Opera prop
31. Pioneer atom splitter
32. Kingfisher's coif
34. ___ de ballet
37. Opposite of hire
38. St. Patrick's home
39. Publicity
45. Conductor Ormandy
46. Analyze verse
47. Skier's site
48. Dietary
49. ___ Point
50. "___ victory!"
51. Stink
52. Substitute
53. Cougar
54. Caddie's offering
55. Home of Jezebel
57. ___ la-la
58. School dance
59. Scottish cap

1	2	3	4	■	5	6	7	8	9	■	10	11	12	13
14				■	15					■	16			
17				18						19				
20			■	21				■	■	22				
■	■	■	23				■	24	25			■	■	■
26	27	28				■	29				■	30	31	32
33				■	■	34					■	35		
36				37	38						39			
40			■	41					■	■	42			
43			■	44				■	45	46				
■	■	■	47				■	48				■	■	■
49	50	51			■	■	52				■	53	54	55
56					57	58					59			
60				■	61					■	62			
63				■	64					■	65			

by Peter (Lefty) Gordon

ACROSS

1. Spirogyra or frog spit
5. Impression
9. Diamond protector
13. Burpee bit
14. Conclude, as negotiations
16. See 31-Across
17. Lefty celebrity relative
20. Turkish title
21. Customary practice
22. Strengthens, with "up"
23. Tugs
25. "Babes in Toyland" star, 1960
28. Head of the costume department?
30. Leonard and Charles
31. With 16-Across, former Phillies manager
34. "Queen ___ Day" (old game show)
35. Corporate abbr.
36. Have a hunch
37. Lefty artist
41. Shows one's humanity
42. Bud
43. ___ Fein
44. Voted
45. Great
46. Overwhelms with humor
48. Catch in a net
50. Pipe type
52. Highest point in Sicily
55. Course for a newcomer to the U.S.: Abbr.
57. Lament
58. Lefty actor
62. French 101 word
63. Copy of a sort
64. Noted rap artist
65. Gloomy
66. Overdecorated
67. Danson et al.

DOWN

1. Composers' org.
2. Three miles, roughly
3. Lefty President
4. Foofaraw
5. Horus's mother
6. Star in Cygnus
7. Baa maid?
8. Razor-billed bird
9. Kind of sax
10. Publican's offerings
11. Ridicule persistently
12. Is worthwhile
15. Lefty actress
18. Five-year periods
19. Refusals
24. Pontiac Silverdome team
26. Camden Yards team
27. Polaroid inventor
29. Lefty comedian
31. Lefty comedian
32. ECU issuer
33. Lawyer in both "Civil Wars" and "L.A. Law"
36. Student's worry
37. Roman law
38. Before, to Byron
39. Jutlander, e.g.
40. In a despicable way
45. Writer Quindlen
47. Blotto
48. $C_4H_{10}O$
49. Subs
51. Bridge seats
52. Horse that made sense?
53. One of the Jackson 5
54. Tannish color
56. Hot
59. Chaperoned girl
60. Actress Joanne
61. Paroxysm

by Jonathan Schmalzbach

ACROSS

1. Scroogian comments
5. Grandson of Adam
9. Biblical possessive
12. Sheltered, at sea
13. Spot for Spartacus
14. Carnival ride cry
15. "Ho, ho, ho" fellow
18. Seems
19. Hockey's Bobby et al.
20. Blue Eagle initials
21. Feasted
23. "My salad days when I was ___": Shakespeare
30. Favorite dog name
31. Closes in on
32. The East
33. Word in a price
35. Volcano spew
36. Deli cry
37. Cause for liniment
38. Not-so-prized fur
40. River inlet
41. Bucky Dent slew it at Fenway Park in 1978
45. Zorba portrayer
46. Tennis call
47. Sulk angrily
48. Many Dickens stories, originally
52. Civil War currency
56. Merit
57. Nintendo hero
58. One of the Simpsons
59. Sot's problem
60. Jot
61. Prepares the dinner table

DOWN

1. Mexican peninsula
2. Crooked
3. Maids
4. Moon goddess
5. Misreckons
6. Born
7. Indivisible
8. ___ Marcos, Tex.
9. Arid region of India
10. Chick watchers
11. Thus far
13. Take with ___ of salt
14. Utility employee
16. It comes in balls
17. Bad news at a talent show
21. "Bull ___" (Costner film)
22. Psyche parts
23. Word in a monarch's name
24. Extent
25. National treasuries
26. Tidy up
27. Teen heartthrob Priestley
28. Undeliverable letter, in post-office talk
29. 13th-century invader
34. Monastery head
38. D.C. legislator
39. El Greco's "View of ___"
42. Nothing: Fr.
43. Pianist Peter
44. Part of rock's C.S.N. & Y.
47. Brotherhood
48. Comic bit
49. "I cannot tell ___"
50. Ultimate
51. Madrid Mmes.
52. Dropout's degree: Abbr.
53. Status letters, perhaps
54. "Say ___"
55. Dernier ___

by Fred Piscop

ACROSS

1. "West Side Story" song
6. 200 milligrams
11. Low island
14. 1968 song "All ___ the Watchtower"
15. River to the Missouri
16. Fuss
17. Seaver's nickname
19. Robert Morse Tony-winning role
20. House cleaner, in England
21. "Absolutely"
22. Legal profession
24. Queen Victoria's house
26. Freight charge
27. Half-wit
28. Better than a bargain
29. Polynesian carvings
33. "Hail, Caesar!"
34. Netman Nastase
37. Sheepish
38. Cup's edge
39. Battery part
40. Anti-prohibitionists
41. Disfigure
42. Get extra life from
43. Portaged
45. Patriotic uncle
47. Rocket's cargo
49. Crib-sheet contents
54. Earthy colors
55. Veneration
56. Hand-cream ingredient
57. "Harper Valley ___"
58. Decorative tree
61. Sock in the jaw
62. Address grandly
63. Coeur d'___, Idaho
64. Flood relief?
65. Pave over
66. Coiffed like Leo

DOWN

1. "Concentration" objective
2. Hello or goodbye
3. Type type
4. Opening
5. Stone, for one
6. Kitchen gadgets
7. Garage-sale words
8. Spitfire fliers, for short
9. Work up
10. Electronics whiz
11. Western spoof of 1965
12. "What ___" ("I'm bored")
13. "___ Sixteen" (Ringo Starr hit)
18. Package-store wares
23. Skater Zayak
25. Place for posies
26. Call back
29. Wrecker
30. "___ had it!"
31. News locale of 12/17/1903
32. Shoe part
33. Auto option, informally
35. Wallet contents, for short
36. Shoebox letters
38. Alan or Cheryl
39. Kind of buildup
41. Gauge
44. Inertia
45. Finn's pal
46. Once again
47. "Where's ___?" (1970 flick)
48. Part owner?
50. Half of a Western city name
51. Pulitzer-winning novelist Glasgow
52. TV exec Arledge
53. Basted
55. Cinema canine
59. ___ out (missed)
60. Descartes's conclusion

by D. J. Listort

ACROSS

1. *Break down grammatically*
6. *Items in a still life*
11. Braincase
13. "___ Fables"
15. Considers bond values again
16. Reduce to ashes
18. Fred's sister
19. ___ Speedwagon
20. Not give ___
21. Mediocre
22. Argued
24. Loudonville, N.Y., campus
25. Classical name in medicine
27. Sprinted
29. "___ Believer" (Monkees hit)
31. Barn topper
32. Football squad
36. Court ruling
37. Hint to solving the eight italicized clues
39. ___ Jima
40. Ignite
42. Plane or dynamic preceder
43. Actress Ryan
44. Deteriorate
45. Curses
47. Sprockets linker
50. Reps.' counterparts
51. Riding whip
55. Natural gait
56. Emily, to Charlotte
57. Madrid attraction
58. Kind of lot
60. Zebralike
62. March laboriously
63. Paired nuclides
64. *Catch suddenly*
65. *Harvests*

DOWN

1. *Trims*
2. Kind of recording
3. Passage ceremony
4. Cash's "A Boy Named ___"
5. Printers' widths
6. Set the standard for
7. Architect Saarinen
8. Chemical suffix
9. Lettuce variety
10. *Bowling save*
11. Tomorrow: Lat.
12. Try again
14. Laurel or Musial
17. Wetlands watchdog
19. Deserters
22. Venus, for one
23. River to the Laptev Sea
24. Game fish
26. 50's singer Frankie
27. Supplies with better weapons
28. Kind
29. ___ tai (cocktail)
30. Cereal bristle
33. Robust energy
34. Pronoun in a cote?
35. Norfolk ale
38. 20 + quires
41. Evaporated
46. Act niggardly
47. Actor Gulager
48. Emcee
49. *Copycats*
50. More extreme
52. *Mustard plants*
53. Baltic Sea feeder
54. Pea places
56. Long account
57. Swift sailing boat
59. B-F connection
60. Salutation for Edmund Hillary
61. Half a fly

54

by Harvey Estes

ACROSS

1. Trounce
8. "My gal" of song
11. Castleberry of "Alice"
14. Have coming
15. Soldier's fare
17. Traveled militarily
18. Catch-22 situation
19. Black and white, e.g.
21. U.S.N. rank
22. Ireland
23. Cosmo and People, e.g.
26. I, to Claudius
27. "___ Lisa"
31. Shower mo.
32. Scruggs of bluegrass
34. Epithet for a tyrant
36. Not a warm welcome
39. Flower child
40. A big blow
41. De Maupassant's "___ Vie"
42. Some of Wordsworth's words
43. Legendary Hollywood monogram
44. Ed of "Daniel Boone"
45. Roller coaster cry
47. "Society's Child" singer Janis ___
49. Sang-froid
56. In progress
57. Vegetarian's no-no
59. Alley of "Look Who's Talking"
60. Rodeo ropes
61. Ship's heading
62. Always, poetically
63. Majority's choice

DOWN

1. S. & L. offerings
2. Lover's ___
3. Christiania, today
4. Scarlett and others
5. Bear Piccolo
6. Civil rights leader Medgar
7. Change the décor
8. Punic War general
9. Knight's attire
10. Slip-up
11. Fight sight
12. Mislay
13. Washington bills
16. Mai ___
20. Like Captain Ahab
23. Like a he-man
24. Sap sucker
25. Bellyache
26. Be off the mark
27. Denver summer time: Abbr.
28. Disgrace
29. Nary a person
30. Saint whose feast day is January 21
32. Biblical judge
33. Word of support
34. Bugs's voice
35. Hairy ancestor
37. Obsolescent disks
38. Engine part
43. Like slim pickings
44. Lacking iron, maybe
45. Essayist E. B.
46. Three-time skating gold medalist
47. Model
48. Novelist Malraux
49. Furnace fuel
50. Getting ___ years
51. Bogeyman
52. Pop music's ___ Lobos
53. Gardner of mysteries
54. Backside
55. Overindulge
58. Chairman's heart?

by David J. Kahn

ACROSS

1. Colo. acad.
5. Start fishing
9. "Dancing Queen" pop group
13. Mata ___
14. Tear to shreds
16. Tactic
17. Singer Antoine from New Orleans
19. Intense anger
20. Carty of baseball
21. ___ and kin
23. "The Company"
24. Mister twister
28. San Francisco area
29. Antitoxins
30. Laughed, in a way
32. Transfer, as a legal proceeding
36. "Tie a Yellow Ribbon" tree
37. Native land
39. Inform (on)
40. Fantasized
44. Durante's "Mrs."
48. Cosmonaut Gagarin
50. 1956 Oscar-winning actress
51. Birthday-suit activity
55. One of L.B.J.'s dogs
56. Munich's river
57. Max or Buddy
59. Till compartment
61. Film hit of 1934
65. Dermatologist's diagnosis
66. Underwater acronym
67. Tevye portrayer on stage
68. Feminist Millett
69. Mikulski and Murkowski: Abbr.
70. Once more

DOWN

1. TV initials
2. Region of heavy W.W. II fighting
3. Heart of the grocery?
4. Champion named 9/1/72
5. ___-Magnon
6. Goal
7. Acerbic
8. Acropolis attire
9. Bank loan abbr.
10. Longtime Supreme Court name
11. Humphrey, to Bacall
12. TV's "___ in the Life"
15. Commotion
18. Act like the Apostle Thomas
22. "___ goes!"
25. ___ Harbour, Fla.
26. Playoff breathers
27. Machine part
28. "___ she blows!"
30. Food fish
31. A dwarf
33. Syracuse players
34. Floral container
35. Biblical suffix
38. Moist
41. Novelist Rand
42. City bond, for short
43. Secret lovefests
45. Appearance at a sit-down?
46. Suspect's "out"
47. Top-rated TV show of the 60's
49. Baking potatoes
51. Kind of therapy
52. Moi's country
53. "___ my case"
54. "Goodnight" girl
58. Steak order
60. Marie, e.g.; Abbr.
62. Aruba product
63. Nolte's "48 ___"
64. Right away

1	2	3	4	■	5	6	7	8	■	■	9	10	11	12
13				■	14				15	■	16			
17				18						■	19			
■	20				■	■	21			22	■	23		
■	■	24			25	26					27			
■	28						■	29				■	■	■
30							31	■	32			33	34	35
36			■	■	■	37		38	■	■	■	39		
40			41	42	43	■	44		45	46	47			
■	■	■	48			49	■	50						■
51	52	53					54						■	■
55			■	56				■	■	57			58	■
59			60	■	61			62	63					64
65				■	66					■	67			
68				■	■	69				■	70			

by Stephanie Spadaccini

ACROSS

1. Caspar or Balthazar, e.g.
6. Rope material
10. Chorale part
14. Florida city
15. Jai ___
16. La Scala presentation
17. NO UNTIDY CLOTHES
20. Walking on air
21. Macadam ingredient
22. ___ Cruces, N.M.
23. Prepared
24. Harem
26. Subordinate Claus
29. Apocalypse
31. Gene material
32. Seldom seen
34. "QB VII" author
36. Lump of jelly, e.g.
39. GOVERN, CLEVER LAD
43. "You said it!"
44. Writer Shere
45. Approve
46. W.W.II grp.
48. Agrippina's son
50. German pronoun
51. Answer to "What's keeping you?"
55. Mount near ancient Troy
57. Item in a lock
58. "I" affliction
59. 1990 Bette Midler film
62. BLATHER SENT ON YE
66. Neighborhood
67. Le Mans, e.g.
68. Conductor Georg
69. Back-to-school time: Abbr.
70. Bouquet
71. Friend of Henry and June

DOWN

1. Word on the Oise
2. Long (for)
3. Food critic Greene
4. Arm bones
5. Fried lightly
6. Actor Charles of "Hill Street Blues"
7. Overhead trains
8. Not shiny
9. A captain of the Enterprise
10. Dance, in France
11. On ___ (doing well)
12. 1979 treaty peninsula
13. Authority
18. Alternate road
19. Los Angeles suburb
24. Obviously pleased
25. Big name in viniculture
26. Physics unit
27. Zhivago's love
28. "It Came ___ Outer Space"
30. Mezz. alternative
33. "It's true," in Torino
35. French resort town
37. Forest florae
38. ___ B'rith
40. Fingernail polish
41. Realism
42. Salon selection
47. Rossini character
49. Potemkin mutiny site
51. Jots
52. Skiing's Phil or Steve
53. Tiptoe
54. Air Force arm: Abbr.
56. Illinois city
59. Cassandra
60. Falana or Montez
61. Opposing
63. Dracula, sometimes
64. Sgt., e.g.
65. Frozen Wasser

1	2	3	4	5	■	6	7	8	9	■	10	11	12	13
14					■	15				■	16			
17					18					19				
■	20						■	21			■	22		
■	■	■	23			■	24				25			
26	27	28	■	29		30		■	31			■	■	■
32			33	■	34			35	■	36		37	38	■
39				40					41					42
■	43				■	44				■	45			
■	■	■	46		47	■	48			49	■	50		
51	52	53				54		■	55		56	■	■	■
57			■	58			■	59				60	61	■
62			63				64							65
66				■	67				■	68				
69				■	70				■	71				

by Mark Danna

ACROSS

1. Actress Winger
6. Park, in Monopoly
11. "Honest" fellow
14. Where Gauguin visited van Gogh
15. Funnyman O'Brien
16. Bloodshot
17. "Cheersl" in Cherbourg?
19. Chang's Siamese twin
20. Brand of lemon-flavored drink
21. Daydream
23. Koch and Wynn
24. Pampering, for short
26. It's heard in a herd
27. Garibaldi in Genoa?
33. Pickle
36. Subject for a supermarket tab
37. Avaricious one
38. October gem
40. Beam fastener
42. 1963 Oscar winner
43. Arose
45. Danger
47. Hang in the breeze
48. Madrid's equivalent of a Texas university?
50. Performance
51. Had lunch
52. Montana and Moon, in brief
55. Gladstone rival
60. Real
62. "Poppycock!"
63. Pre-photo pronouncement in Geneva?
65. Some
66. Skirmish
67. "Dallas" Miss
68. Simonize
69. Classic theater name
70. 4-Down again

DOWN

1. Peri opera
2. Made a boner
3. Post-sneeze word
4. Take money for a spare room
5. Loner
6. Agt.'s share
7. Creator of Lorelei Lee
8. Med. subj.
9. Winter melon
10. Competitor
11. Vicinity
12. Early German carmaker
13. Barely beat, with "out"
18. Woman's top
22. Cartoonist Wilson
25. Islamic leader
28. Crowbar
29. Portugal and its neighbor
30. Barely managed, with "out"
31. Raise
32. Alternative to Charles de Gaulle
33. Clinton's runs
34. Each
35. First name in spying
39. Moon-based
41. Alternative to Certs
44. "Desmoiselles d'Avignon" artist
46. Bloodletting practitioner
49. Potted
52. Put down
53. Count in music
54. Winter weather
55. Extract
56. New Rochelle college
57. Charon's domain
58. Kind of beer
59. Relationship words
61. Prefix with play or scope
64. Favorite relative in politics?

by Harvey Estes

ACROSS

1. Zubin with a baton
6. Old streetlight
13. Daley and others
14. Gravel-voiced actress
15. Iron shortage
16. Commit
17. Just the highlights
18. Slammin' Sam
19. Trendy
20. Getting better, as wine: Var.
22. Up to now
24. Size up
26. Paints amateurishly
28. Almost shut
32. Kind of symbol
33. One whom Jesus healed
34. Rodeo rope
35. Dashboard reading, for short
36. Leave the pier
38. Acquire
39. Ask on one's knees
41. Had
42. Lunch order
43. Belgrade dweller
44. In abeyance
45. Sciences' partner
46. Tooth
48. Comfort
50. Probe
53. Some pads
55. Accident mementos
58. Serves a sentence
60. Byrnes of "77 Sunset Strip"
61. Brown paint, e.g.
62. Six-footer?
63. Resort locale
64. Newspaper section

DOWN

1. Lion's pride?
2. It's hard to miss
3. Respect
4. Nonsense
5. Simile center
6. Comic Kaplan
7. Assuages
8. Picture with its own frame
9. Wheel bolt holder
10. King of comedy
11. Part of a pair
12. Sound of relief
13. Scuff up
14. It's hard to say
18. Fastens with a pop
21. "I have no ___!"
23. ___ chi ch'uan
24. Tail ends
25. Temptation for Atalanta
27. 1991 American Conference champs
29. It's hard
30. Listing
31. Sounds off
33. Digital-watch readout: Abbr.
34. Postal letters
37. Have a hunch
40. 1970 Jackson 5 hit
44. Looking while lusting
45. Waylay
47. Time and again
49. In unison
50. Tots up
51. Afternoon TV fare
52. Lifetime achievement Oscar winner Deborah
54. Mingo portrayer
56. Puerto ___
57. Play place
59. Take part in a biathalon
60. Kipling novel

by Ernie Furtado

ACROSS

1. Swiss city on the Rhine
6. "Jake's Thing" author
10. Nice shindigs
14. Allan-___ (Robin Hood cohort)
15. Carry on
16. "___ Fire" (Springsteen hit)
17. *Paris site*
18. "___ partridge in a . . ."
19. Kind of fountain
20. Runaway, of a sort
22. Runway, of a sort
24. Book-lined rooms
25. *London site*
27. Cartoonist Bushmiller
29. Twofold
32. Game award, for short
35. Make a pot
36. Skin layer
38. *Rome site*
40. *Amsterdam site*
41. Drop out
42. Seat for two or more
43. "You don't ___!"
44. ___-tiller
45. They beat deuces
47. *Florence site*
50. Not on land
54. Upset-minded teams
57. Positions
59. Big 10's ___ State
60. Letter encl.
62. *Moscow site*
63. Derby
64. Ended
65. Off
66. River to the North Sea
67. Corn bread
68. Having an irregular edge

DOWN

1. With ___ breath
2. One of the Astaires
3. Dresden dweller
4. Slip by
5. ___ majesty
6. Mr. Parseghian
7. Sea cow
8. Kipling story locale
9. Legendary Packers QB
10. Surgical knife
11. Love, Spanish-style
12. Italian town, site of a 1796 Napoleon victory
13. Fastener
21. N.F.L. standout Lott
23. Not a main route
26. Naldi of silents
28. 1964 Four Seasons hit
30. "___ 'n' Andy"
31. Trevi Fountain coin
32. Classic sports cars
33. Turn sharply
34. Somewhat, in music
36. Loss
37. High overhead?
39. Money for Mason
40. "Cheers" role
42. Harold of politics
46. Pianist Gyorgy
48. Noted children's writer
49. An encouraging word
51. Defunct treaty org.
52. Group character
53. Unanimously
54. Nimble
55. Birds Eye product
56. ___ over
58. "___ kleine Nachtmusik"
61. Afore

1	2	3	4	5	■	6	7	8	9	■	10	11	12	13
14					■	15				■	16			
17					■	18				■	19			
20					21	■	22			23				
24				■	25	26						■	■	■
■	■	■	27	28				■	■	29		30	31	■
32	33	34	■	35				■	36					37
38			39				■	40						
41						■	42				■	43		
■	44				■	■	45				46	■	■	■
■	■	■	47		48	49				■	50	51	52	53
54	55	56						■	57	58				
59				■	60			61	■	62				
63				■	64				■	65				
66				■	67				■	68				

by Bob Sefick

ACROSS

1. Clicker that might be used on a trawler?
9. London elevator
13. Tibetan V.I.P.
14. Plume source
16. Starter at an Italian restaurant
17. Quick on one's toes
18. Shoshonean
19. Health resort
20. Department store employee
21. Behan's "___ Boy"
23. George Sand, e.g.
24. Gene Kelly's "___ Girls"
25. Loving touches
26. German coal region
28. Propelled a punt
29. Amtrak listing: Abbr.
30. One of the Astors
31. Is interested
32. Caddies carry them
33. Bank account amt.
34. Vatican City dwellers
35. Jetty
36. It causes a reaction
38. Great noise
39. Sparta was its capital
40. Have the chair
44. Resounding, as a canyon
45. TV knob abbr.
46. Statehouse V.I.P.
47. Left the chair
48. Cheese at an Italian restaurant
51. "Put up your ___!"
52. Relinquishes
53. Élan
54. Solemn hymn

DOWN

1. Piece of a poem
2. Change, as hems
3. Capuchin monkey
4. Racetrack informant
5. Confirmation slaps
6. Twangy
7. Ambulance attendant: Abbr.
8. Philosopher's universal
9. Scholarly
10. Eliza's 'enry
11. Chicken dish
12. Distance gauge
13. Paint unskillfully
15. Brewer and Wright
20. Parisian papas
22. Kill, as a dragon
23. Turns white
25. Meltdown areas
26. City south of Palo Alto
27. Salad ingredient
28. ___ New Guinea
30. Throw off the scent
31. Some lose sleep over it
32. Baking pans
34. Most runtlike
35. Polish dumpling
37. Yankee great Skowron et al.
38. Herds
40. Call up
41. Jim Croce's "___ Name"
42. Gift getter
43. Holiday nights
48. Cushion
49. Baseball hitter's stat
50. Household god, in Roman myth

by David Ellis Dickerson

ACROSS

1. Kindergarten instruction
5. Onetime La Scala tenor
11. Shake up
14. Brook
15. Unlocked
16. Hollywood's Thurman
17. Star of "The Invisible Man"
19. Hoover, for one
20. Zeus or Jupiter, e.g.
21. School grp.
22. Wood-shaping tool
23. Fleur-de-___
25. Mr. Sondheim
27. Not left in the lurch
32. "The Time Machine" people
33. Speckled horse
34. Poet Wilfred
36. Meanies
39. Religious offshoot
40. Pay by mail
42. Onetime Texaco rival
43. Not on the level
45. Talkative Barrett
46. Prefix with plasm
47. Not cleric
49. Two-pointer, the hard way
51. Comes out
54. Kin of calypso music
55. Beats it
56. Piggie
58. Orientals, e.g.
63. Belief
64. Star of "The Vanishing" (1993 version)
66. Bedlam site
67. Spoke from the soapbox
68. Pull off a coup
69. Author Beattie
70. Choir voices
71. Minus

DOWN

1. Electrical paths
2. Gyp
3. Ali, once
4. Coin that's not a coin
5. One who shares a masthead billing
6. ___ financing (car ad phrase)
7. Sow's opposite
8. Rightmost column
9. A century in Washington
10. ___ bodkins
11. Star of "Without a Trace"
12. Flabbergast
13. Japanese noodle soup
18. Kewpie
22. Orbiting points
24. Betsy Ross, e.g.
26. "Don't Bring Me Down" rock band
27. Nocturnal bear?
28. They might be heard a thousand times
29. Star of "Missing"
30. All broken up
31. Disband postwar
35. Hirschfeld hides them
37. This, in Madrid
38. Chimney grit
41. Ale mugs
44. Barrister's headgear
48. The "c" in etc.
50. Actress Lemmons
51. "My Fair Lady" lady
52. Stoneworker
53. Divans
57. Newts
59. False god
60. Dickensian chill
61. Eerie loch
62. Concorde et al.
64. Book after Esther
65. A stingy fellow?

by Lois Sidway

ACROSS

1. Whip end
5. Mystery writer's award
10. Sassy young 'un
14. "___ silly question . . ."
15. Painter Andrea del ___
16. Portnoy's creator
17. Hmm?
20. ___ Dame
21. Packwood, for one
22. Curse
25. Purse fastener
26. Jeweler's weight
28. Some of the Brady bunch
31. Eat like a chicken
34. Blend
36. Utah's Hatch
37. D.D.E.'s command
38. Hmm . . .
40. Volga tributary
41. Writer Terkel
43. Requisite
44. Porch adjunct
45. Arab capital
46. Ignoramus
48. South African statesman Jan
51. Gospel singer Jackson
55. Many TV shows
57. Cathedral displays
58. Hmm!
61. Mitch Miller's instrument
62. Mountain nymph
63. Electricity carrier
64. District
65. Don Knotts won five
66. Actress Young

DOWN

1. Suburban greenery
2. Seeing ___ (since)
3. Do figure eights
4. Where to hang your chapeau
5. Biblical verb ending
6. "Zip-a-Dee-Doo-___"
7. Alum
8. Relics collect here
9. The "R" in H.R.H.
10. Pugilistic muscleman
11. Famous debater
12. Rat chaser?
13. Talese's "Honor ___ Father"
18. Word repeated after "Que"
19. Speaker
23. In a line
24. Eagle's nail
27. Like Neptune's trident
29. Adidas rival
30. Break sharply
31. Annoyance
32. Famous last words
33. Camp V.I.P.
35. Concert hall
38. Debate subjects
39. Irish novelist O'Brien
42. Like a golf ball
44. Manatees
47. Word sung twice before "cheree"
49. Lake near Carson City
50. Drang's partner
52. DeVito's "Taxi" role
53. Venous opening
54. Gray
55. Ms. McEntire
56. Cherry leftover
58. "Far out!"
59. Spring time
60. Gains for O. J.

1	2	3	4	■	5	6	7	8	9	■	10	11	12	13
14				■	15					■	16			
17				18						19				
20					■	■	21							■
22					23	24	■	25					■	■
■	■	■	26				27	■	■	28			29	30
31	32	33		■	34			35	■	36				
37			■	38					39		■	40		
41			42		■	43				■	44			
45					■	■	46			47		■	■	■
■	■	48			49	50	■	51				52	53	54
■	55						56	■	■	57				
58								59	60					
61				■	62					■	63			
64				■	65					■	66			

by David Ellis Dickerson

ACROSS

1. Masquerades
6. "Fe, fi, fo, ___!"
9. Batman foe, with "The"
14. Native Alaskan
15. Prince Hirobumi
16. Sheeplike
17. Irving's "A Prayer for Owen ___"
18. The lambada, once
19. Grand mountain
20. Dr. Seuss title
23. Actress Skye
24. Ho Chi ___
25. Car job
28. ___ Bingle (Crosby)
30. God Almighty
34. A year in Mexico
35. Put to the grindstone
37. Studio prop
38. Dr. Seuss title
41. Plant seeds again.
42. ___-scarum
43. Coach Parseghian
44. Shakespearean oath
46. Smidgen
47. Love of Greece?
48. Dance or hairstyle
50. Calf's meat
52. Dr. Seuss title
59. One-___ (short play)
60. Crystal ball, e.g.
61. Keep busy
62. Violinist Isaac
63. Part of R.S.V.P.
64. Wrestling's late ___ the Giant
65. Western film title of '75 and '93
66. Golf peg
67. Relaxes

DOWN

1. Like venison
2. Out of the wind
3. Carroll contemporary
4. Em, e.g.
5. Pen, for Pierre
6. About mid-month, with "the"
7. Brigham Young's home
8. Computer-phone link
9. Norse land of giants
10. Make out at a party?
11. Songstress Eartha
12. Organic compound
13. Philosopher Descartes
21. Conclude with
22. Small bird
25. Dens
26. Hungry
27. Idaho city
29. Betty Ford program
31. 1991 Stallone comedy
32. Brain surgeon's prefix
33. Columnist Maxwell et al.
35. Author from Salem, Mass.
36. Inferable
39. Dinner chickens
40. More like Shirley Temple
45. ___ Solo of "Star Wars"
47. Sir Galahad's mother
49. Popular word game
51. "___ is Born"
52. Fastener
53. VIII, to Virgil
54. Blvds. and rds.
55. Toledo's vista
56. Hitches
57. William of "The Doctor"
58. Unlocks, in a sonnet

1	2	3	4	5	■	6	7	8	■	9	10	11	12	13
14					■	15			■	16				
17					■	18			■	19				
20					21				22					
■	■	■	23				■	24				■	■	■
25	26	27		■	28		29	■	30			31	32	33
34			■	35				36	■	37				
38			39						40					
41					■	42					■	43		
44					45	■	46			■	47			
■	■	■	48			49	■	50		51		■	■	■
52	53	54					55					56	57	58
59					■	60			■	61				
62					■	63			■	64				
65					■	66			■	67				

by Harvey Estes

ACROSS
1. On the ___ (very angry)
8. For the well-to-do
15. November winner
16. Savannah's place
17. "Evil Ways" band
18. Bar members
19. Dynamite's kin
20. Christian Science founder
22. Pope's "An ___ on Man"
23. ___ way (incidentally)
25. Murals and the like
26. Free-for-all
29. Play callers
31. Ill-fated sibling rival
35. Put on a pedestal
36. Ark builder
37. Singer Falana
38. String player
40. "Hop to it!"
42. Cancer's symbol
43. Reds' Rose
45. 2:1, e.g.
46. "A-one and ___"
47. "I smell ___"
48. TV pitchman Merlin
49. "A Christmas Carol" boy
51. Student of optometry?
53. Edinburgh dwellers
56. Aloe ___ (lotion ingredient)
57. Retirement kitty, for short
60. Evangeline, e.g.
62. Last-place finisher, so it's said
65. Unyielding
66. Fence in
67. Reneges
68. Quotes poetry

DOWN
1. Frontierward
2. Chester Arthur's middle name
3. Monthly due
4. %: Abbr.
5. ___ loss for words
6. Belief
7. Edith + Holly
8. Hideous
9. Black-eyed one, perhaps
10. Farmer, in the spring
11. Billy + Lucille
12. "Rock of ___"
13. Italian bread
14. Word before come and go
21. Car for test-driving
23. Alexander + Timothy
24. Abominable Snowman
25. Tennis's Arthur
26. Islamic center
27. Bring to bear
28. Steven Bochco TV drama
30. Patti + Lana
32. Boxing matches
33. Borden bovine
34. Instructions to Macduff
39. Lunch meat
41. "Star Trek" counselor
44. Record
50. Basketball's Thomas
52. "Common Sense" author
53. "Saint Joan" playwright
54. Sign over
55. Reverend Roberts
56. Animal docs
57. "___ You Babe"
58. Misleading move
59. Senate votes
61. SSW's reverse
63. New Deal grp.
64. Yale player

by Arthur S. Ash

ACROSS

1. Razor sharpener
6. Health resort
9. More than a mere success
14. Mussolini's notorious son-in-law
15. Assist
16. With uneven gait
17. Mink's poor cousin
18. Ushered
19. Truism
20. Item to cut for dessert
23. Late-night star
24. President Manuel, ousted by Franco
25. TV rooms
26. New Rochelle institution
28. Game show sound
30. Princess Diana's family name
33. Bedecked
37. Mea ___
38. Get repeated value from
39. Replaceable shoe parts
42. Agrees
44. Carry on
45. 30's and 40's actress Anna
46. Porcine cry
49. Kind of system
51. Weakens
55. Popular poultry entree
58. ___ hilt (fully)
59. "Le veau ___" ("Faust" aria)
60. Roomy dress cut
61. Chef's attire
62. Consume
63. Noted name in Bosnian talks
64. Oceans, to Longfellow
65. Season on the Riviera
66. Lawn tool

DOWN

1. "Bad mood" look
2. Small obligation
3. Snitch about
4. Entree for a solitary diner
5. Scrutinize, with "over"
6. Marathoner Alberto
7. Michelangelo work
8. Afterthoughts
9. Bridge desideratum
10. Dieter's dish
11. A miss's equivalent
12. Dish's companion in flight
13. Songs of glory
21. Diminish
22. Foray
27. Florida city
29. Like Eric the Red
30. H.S. subject
31. So-called "lowest form of wit"
32. Bygone trains
34. Sally Field TV role
35. Erhard's training
36. ___ Plaines, Ill.
40. Prefer follower
41. Latecomer to a theater, maybe
42. Ancient fertility goddess
43. Suffix with young or old
46. Santa's reindeer, e.g.
47. "___ you're happy!"
48. Potassium salt
50. Summer ermine
52. Geriatric process
53. ___ de León
54. Lip curl
56. Understands
57. Pan's opposite

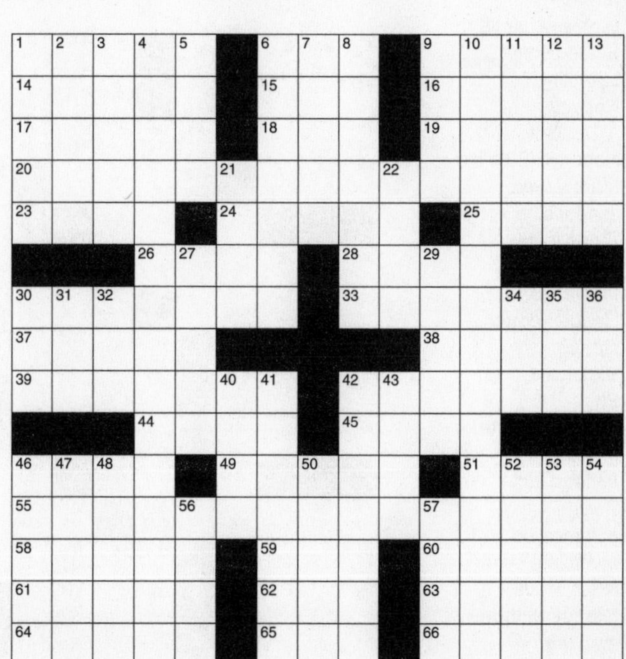

by Roger H. Courtney

ACROSS
1. Cremona violinmaker
6. Henri's squeeze
10. Tennis units
14. Quarrel
15. Stadium protests
16. Wynken, Blynken and Nod, e.g.
17. Criticize a prizefight?
19. Small brook
20. Transgression
21. Blackmailed
22. Cold stick
24. Le Sage's "Gil ___"
25. One way to run
26. Instruments for Rostropovich
29. Economic hostility
33. Poet T. S.
34. Trumpeter Al
35. ___ morgana (mirage)
36. Highway caution
37. Skater Sonja
38. Late king of Norway
39. "I ___ Got Nobody" (20's hit)
40. Mare's feed
41. Jacques, in song
42. Rings loudly
44. Bell's signal
45. Itineraries: Abbr.
46. Handed-down stories
47. Expensive
50. Bit
51. Word with date or process
54. Imitator Little
55. Boxing commission?
58. Medicinal plant
59. Killer whale
60. "Happy Birthday" medium
61. Cravings
62. Shade of blue
63. Cup of thé

DOWN
1. Clumsy boats
2. Actor Paul
3. Ever and ___
4. Idiosyncrasy
5. Imagination tester
6. French clergymen
7. "___ Indigo"
8. Chit
9. Guesswork
10. How hard Riddick Bowe can hit?
11. Rock star Clapton
12. Cash drawer
13. Fileted fish
18. "What a pity!"
23. Delivery letters
24. Items used in "light" boxing?
25. "Mrs. ___ Goes to Paris"
26. Actor Romero
27. "Dallas" matriarch Miss ___
28. Detroit footballers
29. Hues
30. Charles's princedom
31. Old name in game arcades
32. "Nevermore" quoter
34. Call at a coin flip
37. Winnie-the-pooh receptacle
41. Awhile
43. Shoshonean
44. Humorist Lazlo
46. Not an express
47. Devoutly wish
48. Annoy
49. Religious image
50. Peruvian Indian
51. Speaker's spot
52. Coffee dispensers
53. Fisher's "Postcards From the ___"
56. Suffix with fail
57. Wood sorrel

by Ernie Furtado

ACROSS

1. Dogpatch's creator
5. Palindromic term of address
9. Talked, old-style
14. Nose tweaker
15. Willa Cather's "One of ___"
16. With sickly pallor
17. Dream
18. Till's bills
19. Rags-to-riches writer
20. Start of an old motto
22. List ender
23. Shooter ammo
24. Part 2 of motto
26. Take ___ (accompaniers)
29. ___ of one's own medicine
30. Part 3 of motto
31. Bulldog
32. Twosome
36. Martinique, e.g.
37. Environmentally minded, for short
39. Hook shape
41. "Don't Bring Me Down" rock group
42. Miami's county
44. Blanche in "The Golden Girls"
46. Part 4 of motto
48. Particle
50. Conquering hero
51. Part 5 of motto
54. Aerialist's safeguard
55. Theater people
56. End of motto
61. Sightseeing sight
62. Golfer Isao ___
63. Singleton
64. Ball
65. A night in Paris
66. Exterior: Prefix
67. Blackthorn shrubs
68. 1949 erupter
69. Creep through the cracks

DOWN

1. Search thoroughly
2. Together, musically
3. On hold
4. Make believe
5. Heath
6. Godmother, often
7. Rings of color
8. Orig. texts
9. Mower's trails
10. Mouth parts
11. White, informally
12. Last name in fashion
13. Nest for 21-Down: Var.
21. See 13-Down
22. "Me" types
25. Thumb-twiddling
26. Fatty ___
27. Refrain part
28. 1985 Danielle Steel best seller
33. Regretfulness
34. Choir voice
35. Koh-i-___ (famed diamond)
38. Pinch reaction
40. Cut of meat
43. Nitty-gritty
45. Just managed
47. Streets
49. Medea's ill-fated uncle
51. Miss Muffet edible
52. Business as ___
53. Zoo heavyweight
57. Related
58. Comic Rudner
59. Spot
60. "Avast!"
62. Actress Sue ___ Langdon

1	2	3	4	■	5	6	7	8	■	9	10	11	12	13
14				■	15				■	16				
17				■	18				■	19				
20				21				■	22					
■	■	23			■	■	24	25						
26	27				28	■	29					■	■	■
30						■	31			■	32	33	34	35
36			■	37		38	■	39		40	■	41		
42			43	■	44		45	■	46		47			
■	■	■	48	49				■	50					
51	52	53						■	■	54			■	■
55						■	56	57	58				59	60
61					■	62				■	63			
64					■	65				■	66			
67					■	68				■	69			

by Jonathan Schmalzbach

ACROSS

1. Mercury or Mars
4. Good old boy
9. Double crosser
14. 1979 film "Norma ___"
15. W.W. I battle site
16. Pomme de ___ (French potato)
17. Modern bank "employee": Abbr.
18. "___ in Venice"
19. Feeling regret
20. Night photographer's work, with "a"?
23. Common connectors
24. Bother
25. Wears well
27. Kind of budget
32. Dustin, in "Midnight Cowboy"
33. Actress Ward of "Sisters"
34. Exist
35. Like an inept photographer's subject?
39. Christina's dad
40. Snoop Doggy Dogg songs
41. Ploys
42. Indy and Daytona
45. Classified
46. Sleep stage: Abbr.
47. Family member
48. Photojournalists' choices?
54. "___ Paradiso" (1966 film)
56. Catalyst
57. Mining area
58. "___ of robins in her hair"
59. San ___, Calif.
60. Chemical suffix
61. Mill, to a cent
62. Embellish
63. ___ Guinea

DOWN

1. Fat, in France
2. Vow
3. Floor model
4. Owing to
5. Defeats
6. Imps
7. One of the March sisters
8. Netman Arthur
9. Road, in Roma
10. Reflex messenger
11. Composer Satie
12. Prince Valiant's son
13. Fraternity party staple
21. "Jerusalem Delivered" poet
22. ___ Lama
25. Author Esquivel
26. Greek
27. Computer sounds
28. Swiss range
29. Trigger
30. Fumbled
31. Grades below the curve
32. Surf sound
33. Open carriage
36. Chaplin persona
37. Shadow-y surname?
38. ___-frutti
43. One of the Gallos
44. Affluence
45. Spoiler
47. Vinegar: Prefix
48. British gun
49. Lady of Spain
50. "Holy moly!"
51. Unrestricted
52. Supreme Court complement
53. Brood
54. Topper
55. Single

by Betty Jorgensen

ACROSS
1. Incarcerate
5. Wife, in Madrid
11. U.S./U.K. divider
14. Wearer of an aiguillette
15. Warehouse charge
17. Start of a quip
19. Slippery swimmer
20. Axis end
21. Lift, as ice or oysters
22. Ilk
23. Enormous
26. Stress
29. "McSorley's Bar" painter John
30. Good earth
31. New Zealand native
32. Family V.I.P.'s
35. Middle of the quip
39. Pigpen
40. Brainy group
41. Something to cop
42. Mork's gal
43. Like schlock
45. Extra leaves
48. Ireland's ___ Islands
49. Spread for a spread
50. Manchurian border river
51. Sunny day production
54. End of the quip
59. Starlet's hope
60. Lackawanna's partner in railroads
61. Draft agcy.
62. Dallas's ___ Plaza
63. Become tiresome

DOWN
1. Rib
2. Yorkshire river
3. Worshiped one
4. Rock's ___ Zeppelin
5. Police accompaniment
6. Clown's prop
7. Corn bread
8. Assn.
9. Writer Rohmer
10. Farming: Abbr.
11. "Flow gently, sweet ___": Burns
12. Coming-of-age period
13. Shelf
16. Consumed
18. "___ the Roof" (1963 hit)
22. It's good for the long haul
23. Actress Massey
24. Filipino
25. Hotel housekeeper
26. Pauper's cry
27. Old feller
28. Guinea pig
29. Impertinent
31. Obeys
32. House slipper
33. Lincoln and Vigoda
34. Dog command
36. Head of Abu Dhabi
37. Shipped
38. Unguarded, as a receiver
42. Reagan Attorney General
43. Like a curmudgeon
44. Mata ___
45. Bridge declaration
46. D.E.A. workers
47. Swizzles
48. Provide divertissement
50. Soviet spy Rudolf
51. Now's partner
52. Siberia's site
53. River of Flanders
55. Proof's ending
56. Half of deux
57. Seventh Greek letter
58. Like a crescent moon

by Jonathan Schmalzbach

ACROSS

1. Send a Dear John letter
5. Antarctica's ___ Coast
10. Stain on Santa
14. Medicinal herb
15. "Golden" song
16. Transportation Secretary Federico
17. Prefix with bucks or bytes
18. Ad: Part 1
20. Ad: Part 2
22. And others
23. Lennon's lady
24. Clinches
25. Ad: Part 3
28. Ad: Part 4
33. Beats
34. Judge
35. Dogpatch diminutive
36. Cabbies' credentials: Abbr.
37. Jabbed
38. Radio knob
39. And so forth, for short
40. Singular person
41. Gladiator's place
42. Medium in which this puzzle's ad appeared
45. Furnishes for a time
46. Twilights, poetically
47. Richmond was its cap.
48. Queen Victoria's husband
51. Ad: Part 5
55. Sponsor of the ad
57. Snead and Spade
59. 15 miles of song
60. Floor pieces
61. Wasatch Range state
62. Prepared to drive
63. Unclogs
64. Glazier's section

DOWN

1. Predicament
2. "___ a song go . . ."
3. CBS's eye, e.g.
4. Genteel snack spots
5. Topper's first name
6. Wings
7. Peculiar: Prefix
8. Clear
9. Downcast
10. Quite an impression
11. Trompe l'___
12. "Dedicated to the ___ Love"
13. Noted Chaplin follower
19. Shoshoneans
21. Responsibility
24. Buries
25. Shiftless one
26. ___ Bandito of commercials
27. New Mexico's state flower
28. Offenses
29. "The Old ___ Bucket"
30. Martian or Venusian
31. Article of food
32. Actress Raines and others
37. Indicates
38. Concocts
41. In addition
43. Adjudged
44. "Buona ___" (Italian greeting)
47. Judit Polgar's game
48. Help a crook
49. Bait
50. Spreadable cheese
51. Tempest
52. Browning locale
53. "Do I dare to ___ peach?": Eliot
54. Muscat's land
56. Fashionable
58. That girl

by Raymond Hamel

ACROSS

1. "St. John Passion" composer
5. In vogue
9. Carpet variety
13. Nepal's location
14. Leftovers dish
15. Prowess
16. "Lost Horizon" paradise
18. Public sentiment
19. "Message received"
20. Songwriter John
21. Long, deep bow
25. More than a snack
27. First look
30. 1901 Churchill novel, with "The"
34. With masts fully extended
35. Imprint on glass
37. Posted
38. Puny pup
39. Dweller in Gulliver's Houyhnhnmland
40. Wash
41. Deuce topper
42. Skater Heiden
43. Idolater
44. Snow remover?
46. Seven Cities of Cibola seeker
48. George Takei TV/movie role
50. Confuses
51. Shore bird
54. Soprano Nixon
57. Dik Browne Viking
58. Town visited by Tommy Albright
63. Subtle twist
64. Like elbowing, e.g.
65. Paris landing site
66. Aromatic herb
67. Prepared brandy
68. Start for "of honor" or "of silence"

DOWN

1. ___ relief
2. Ski wood
3. "The Company"
4. Solo of "Star Wars"
5. Plating material
6. Nixon chief of staff
7. Sunny vacation spot
8. Mojo
9. King Kong's home
10. Saber handle
11. To boot
12. ___ Burnie, Md.
15. Aborigine's weapon
17. Woodworker's concern
21. City attacked by Cleon
22. Fabric with a raised pattern
23. Near ringer
24. "Jaws" locale
26. Canyon sound
28. Bring up
29. Work ___
31. Action star Steven
32. Blitz
33. Typing pool members
36. Designer Chanel
39. Make oneself heard in the din
43. Lecterns
45. "Tumbling Tumbleweeds" singer, 1935
47. Traveled far and wide
49. Eclipse shadow
51. Kind of splints
52. Butler's quarters?
53. Operatic prince
55. ". . . as a bug in ___"
56. Sally of NASA
59. Medic
60. Spanish gold
61. Timeworn
62. TV comic Louis

by Charles Arnold

ACROSS

1. Guzzles
7. Bebop
11. Certain muscles, informally
14. Dislocate
15. Woodwind
16. Varnish resin
17. Ancient ascetic
18. Letter writing: Abbr.
19. Japanese admiral Yuko
20. Battleship
23. Mesmerized
27. "Or ___!" (veiled threat)
28. "Torero Saluting" painter
29. Rioting
31. Despicable
32. Greek market
33. Mitigates
35. Actor Matheson or Allen
38. Dictionary
40. Rogers's partner
42. Wily
43. Topple
45. Fudd of cartoondom
46. Director's cry
47. Bee activity
49. ___ Downs (English race track)
52. Contented sound
53. ___ fixe
54. Bluff, with a gun
57. Nuclear defense grp.
58. Russia's ___ Mountains
59. Slanted
64. Petition
65. Scoop (out)
66. To wit
67. "___! We Have No Bananas"
68. Whirlpool
69. Like Parmesan

DOWN

1. Neighbor of Ont.
2. Raises
3. "___ Gratis Artis" (M-G-M motto)
4. Enemy
5. Dear, as memories
6. Two-track
7. Oedipus's mother
8. Lodging
9. Swedish painter of "At the Granary Door"
10. "Fiddler on the Roof" star
11. Straighten
12. Wash up
13. "Waverley" novelist
21. Burstyn and Barkin
22. Labor org.
23. Iranian dollars
24. Theater backer
25. Stand-in
26. Actress Garr
30. Transistor predecessor
31. "___ Misérables"
34. Cronus, to Romans
35. Meek
36. "*The* woman" for Sherlock
37. Traffic sign
39. Choose
41. Prefix with meter
44. Just as much
46. Bill's partner
48. Vexing
49. Emerson piece
50. Aspect
51. Noted White House resident
52. Multicolored pattern
55. Slender nail
56. Sirius, e.g.
60. Drs.' org.
61. Tennis call
62. ___ de France
63. Dancer Charisse

by Christopher Hurt

ACROSS

1. Greatly impressed
5. Chairman ___
8. Poet Mandelstam
12. Charming
15. Viper
16. Moore of "A Few Good Men"
17. Sagan's "___ Brain"
18. 40-Across's beloved 11
20. Shifty shoe?
22. African nation since 1993
23. Danger
25. Reps.
26. Close, as friends
29. Musician's job
31. Composer of "Socrate"
34. National park in Maine
36. Shem's father
38. Getting on
39. Indian writer Santha Rama ___
40. Theme of this puzzle
42. End up ahead
43. Frank Baum's initial initial
44. Angel's headgear
45. California's motto
47. Hebrew master
49. Dutch airline
51. Spinners, e.g.
52. Brain tests, for short
54. Essentials
56. Common speech
59. Bureau
63. Locale of 40-Across
65. Mourn
66. Prolific "author"
67. ___ pro nobis
68. Plains Indians
69. Items in a code
70. ___ Luthor
71. Boss Tweed lampooner

DOWN

1. Liturgical robes
2. Eroded
3. Bacchanalian cry
4. Crab, e.g.
5. Small rug
6. Late tennis great
7. It may be seria or buffa
8. Single-named folk singer
9. 40-Across landmark
10. Hungary's Nagy
11. Galileo's home
13. 40-Across's eastern border
14. Belgian river
19. Feature of 40-Across, according to Sandburg
21. Get-up
24. 1860 nominee in 40-Across
26. Less cluttered
27. Florida city
28. 1976 Nobel Prize winner from 40-Across
30. Indian district
32. "___ Ike" (50's slogan)
33. Millay and Ferber
35. Cry of discovery
37. Ripen
41. Kind
46. Type of roulette
48. Sets sail
50. Avg.
53. Pub perch
55. Therefore
56. Perfume holder
57. Humerus neighbor
58. Mary Robinson's land
60. Nintendo rival
61. Impending times
62. "Give it a ___"
64. Wailing instrument

by Joan Yanofsky

ACROSS

1. Petite or jumbo
5. Gobs
9. Final Four rounds
14. Composer Satie
15. ___ avail
16. Gather into folds
17. Fashionable African land?
19. Chain of hills
20. Till compartment
21. Tartarus captive, in myth
22. Military encounter
25. ___ projection (map system)
27. Escargots
28. Embarrassment
30. Accede (to)
31. Places of refuge
32. Neither's partner
34. "The Twilight of the ___"
35. Unites
36. Deal (out)
37. ___ Lanka
38. Birdie beater
39. "Give My Regards to Broadway" composer
40. Meeting musts
42. "Canterbury Tales" Inn
43. Gabriel, e.g.
44. Curmudgeon-like
45. Composer Duparc
47. Courts
48. "___ Cowboy"
49. Fashionable state?
54. Enact
55. Zone
56. Arched recess
57. "Flowers for Algernon" author Daniel
58. ". . . leave no ___ unstoned"
59. Haydn's "Nelson," for one

DOWN

1. Wine description
2. George's lyricist brother
3. Address part
4. ___ out a living
5. Some temps
6. "Two Women" Oscar winner
7. Remnants
8. Tale of ___
9. Naiads' homes
10. Donizetti's "The ___ of Love"
11. Fashionable Canadian city?
12. "Othello" villain
13. Actress Anna
18. Curtain fabric
22. Silky-haired cat
23. Fashionable Welsh body of water?
24. Bonds
25. Scold
26. Rest on one's ___
27. Is weary
28. Summons
29. Person with a seal
31. Kind of tender
33. Rip
35. 1977 Wimbledon champ
36. Crowds around
38. Turbojet and others
39. Movement
41. Infuriate
42. Paris or Hector
44. Cringe
45. Corn covering
46. Russian-born designer
47. "___ off to see"
49. King Cole
50. Computer capacity, for short
51. Site of rejuvenation
52. Double twist
53. "You bet!"

by Arthur S. Verdesca

ACROSS

1. Yin's partner
5. Toy gun ammo
9. Rift
14. ___ patriae (patriotism)
15. Together, in music
16. "It ___ Be You"
17. Parisian entree
18. Vatican City monetary unit
19. Down Under soldier
20. 1954 Hitchcock hit
23. Bonny one
24. Singer Acuff
25. Beautify
28. Barley bristle
30. Buddy
34. Spanish wave
35. Passage
37. Cain's nephew
38. Behave
42. Clam supper
43. Sacred song
44. Onetime medicinal herb
45. German donkey
46. Élan
47. Charitable foundations, e.g.
49. Chinese ideal
51. Part of a wagon train
52. Merit award
59. Use
60. Candy brand
61. Paint unskillfully
62. Mesa ___ National Park
63. Felipe, Jesus or Matty
64. Former Mormon chief ___ Taft Benson
65. Shipping amount
66. Desires
67. ___ Bien Phu (1954 battle site)

DOWN

1. Croquet locale
2. French call for help
3. ___ cloud in the sky
4. Edsel feature
5. Soft leather
6. Farewell
7. Result of tummy rubbing?
8. Ore layer
9. Maria Rosario Pilar Martinez
10. Jacks-of-all-trades
11. Wood trimmer
12. Weekly World News rival
13. Beaded shoe, for short
21. Chinese-Portuguese enclave
22. Coffee server
25. Ice cream mold
26. Biblical prophet
27. Thanks, in Thüringen
28. Journalist Joseph
29. Grieved
31. "My Dinner With ___"
32. Brimless hat
33. Test car maneuvers
36. 18-wheeler
39. Iron pumper's pride
40. Diligent
41. Lagoon former
46. Actress Caldwell
48. Lacked
50. Locale in van Gogh paintings
51. Breakfast fruit
52. At any time
53. Betting game
54. Kind of vision
55. Fiddlers' king
56. "Schindler's List" extra
57. Fix
58. Israeli diplomat
59. Dow Jones fig.

1

G	O	T		O	V	A	L	S		R	A	T	S	O
A	N	A		A	I	M	E	E		O	T	H	E	R
L	E	I		H	O	P	O	M	Y	T	H	U	M	B
L	A	W	F	U	L		N	I	E	C	E			
I	T	A	L			C	A	S	S		N	A	V	E
C	A	N	A	S	T	A				H	A	C	E	K
			S	T	A	R	D	A	T	E		L	Y	E
		S	K	I	P	T	O	M	Y	L	O	U		
A	L	E		R	E	A	S	O	N	E	R			
P	E	R	M	S				R	E	N	D	E	R	S
T	O	F	U		M	A	M	E			E	L	A	N
			P	I	E	T	A		H	O	R	A	C	E
J	U	M	P	S	T	A	R	T	E	D		I	K	E
A	G	R	E	E		L	I	K	E	D		N	E	Z
W	H	I	T	E		L	O	O	P	S		E	R	E

2

S	E	L	F		G	A	G	S			P	E	L	E
O	V	A	L		A	C	R	E	S		L	A	O	S
F	I	R	E	E	S	C	A	P	E		U	R	G	E
A	L	D	E	N			N	I	C	E	S	T		
			S	I	R		D	A	T	E		H	O	R
O	A	S		D	E	S	I			L	I	M	B	O
C	L	U	B		C	O	L	O	R		T	O	L	D
U	L	N	A		A	L	O	N	E		E	V	A	N
L	U	G	S		P	I	Q	U	E		M	E	T	E
A	R	L	E	S			U	S	S	R		R	E	Y
R	E	A		A	S	H	E		E	O	S			
		S	A	T	E	E	N			O	P	E	R	A
G	A	S	P		W	A	T	E	R	M	E	L	O	N
A	G	E	S		S	P	L	I	T		L	I	S	T
P	O	S	E			S	Y	N	E		L	E	S	S

3

B	A	L	D		C	O	E	D			P	E	N	N
A	L	I	E		O	R	L	E		L	E	V	E	E
R	O	B	S		L	A	I	T		I	N	E	R	T
B	U	R	E	A	U		H	A	R	V	A	R	D	
	D	A	R	T	M	O	U	T	H					
			T	A	B	U			O	R	N	E	R	Y
D	E	M			I	T	L	L		I	O	N	I	A
I	V	Y	L	E	A	G	U	E	S	C	H	O	O	L
V	I	R	A	L		O	V	A	L			S	S	E
A	L	A	S	K	A			R	I	B	S			
					P	R	I	N	C	E	T	O	N	
	C	O	R	N	E	L	L		K	E	E	P	U	P
S	A	M	O	A		E	L	L	E		P	E	K	E
B	R	O	W	N		S	U	E	R		P	R	E	P
A	D	O	S			S	S	T	S		E	A	S	E

4

E	C	H	O		Y	O	G	A		H	U	M	I	D
C	L	O	D		E	V	E	N		U	T	I	C	A
L	A	R	D		M	E	T	S		D	A	R	E	D
A	S	S		J	E	R	S	E	Y	S	H	O	R	E
T	H	E	C	A	N			L	E	O				
		R	O	P	I	N	G		A	N	S	W	E	R
O	M	A	H	A		A	L	A	R		T	H	R	U
P	O	C	O	N	O	M	O	U	N	T	A	I	N	S
A	V	E	R		N	E	W	T		R	I	T	E	S
L	E	S	T	W	E		S	O	F	I	N	E		
				R	A	E			U	P	S	H	O	T
T	H	E	H	A	M	P	T	O	N	S		O	W	E
A	U	R	I	C		C	O	R	N		L	U	N	D
F	L	I	C	K		O	N	C	E		U	S	E	D
T	A	N	K	S		T	E	A	L		V	E	R	Y

5

L	A	D	D		R	I	V	E	R		C	H	E	R
A	W	A	Y		E	M	I	L	E		L	I	V	E
M	A	N	E	E	V	E	N	T	S		A	R	I	A
A	R	E		L	I	T		O	I	L	W	E	L	L
S	E	S	A	M	E		A	N	N	I	E			
			I	O	W	A	N		S	E	D	A	T	E
W	E	A	R		E	X	E	S		S	M	I	R	K
A	L	D	A		D	E	M	O	S		O	D	I	E
F	L	A	P	S		S	O	F	T		N	A	P	S
T	E	M	P	U	S		N	A	I	V	E			
			A	M	P	L	E		N	I	T	W	I	T
S	C	O	R	P	I	O		A	K	A		O	R	E
L	O	V	E		C	R	E	W	E	L	H	O	A	X
O	M	E	N		E	N	T	E	R		B	E	T	A
B	E	R	T		S	E	E	D	S		O	D	E	S

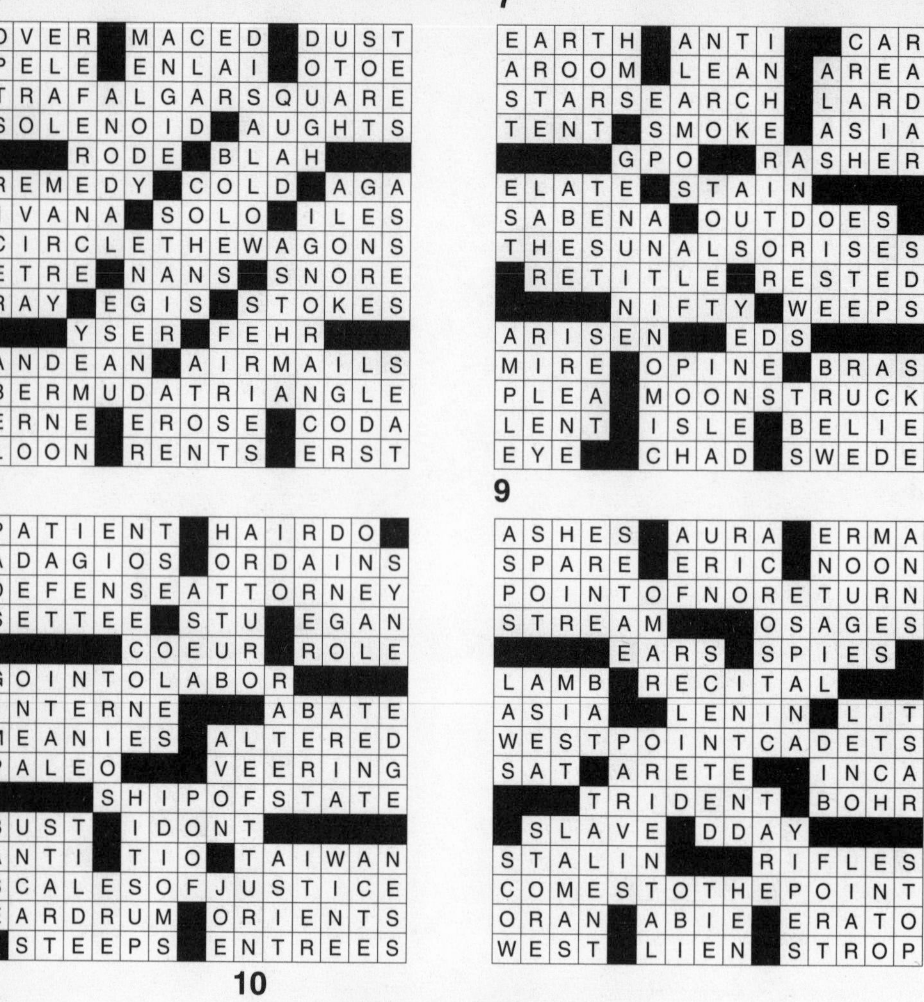

6

OVER MACED DUST
PELE ENLAI OTOE
TRAFALGARSQUARE
SOLENOID AUGHTS
RODE BLAH
REMEDY COLD AGA
IVANA SOLO ILES
CIRCLETHEWAGONS
ETRE NANS SNORE
RAY EGIS STOKES
YSER FEHR
ANDEAN AIRMAILS
BERMUDATRIANGLE
ERNE EROSE CODA
LOON RENTS ERST

7

EARTH ANTI CAR
AROOM LEAN AREA
STARSEARCH LARD
TENT SMOKE ASIA
GPO RASHER
ELATE STAIN
SABENA OUTDOES
THESUNALSORISES
RETITLE RESTED
NIFTY WEEPS
ARISEN EDS
MIRE OPINE BRAS
PLEA MOONSTRUCK
LENT ISLE BELIE
EYE CHAD SWEDE

8

PATIENT HAIRDO
ADAGIOS ORDAINS
DEFENSEATTORNEY
SETTEE STU EGAN
COEUR ROLE
GOINTOLABOR
INTERNE ABATE
MEANIES ALTERED
PALEO VEERING
SHIPOFSTATE
BUST IDONT
ANTI TIO TAIWAN
SCALESOFJUSTICE
EARDRUM ORIENTS
STEEPS ENTREES

9

ASHES AURA ERMA
SPARE ERIC NOON
POINTOFNORETURN
STREAM OSAGES
EARS SPIES
LAMB RECITAL
ASIA LENIN LIT
WESTPOINTCADETS
SAT ARETE INCA
TRIDENT BOHR
SLAVE DDAY
STALIN RIFLES
COMESTOTHEPOINT
ORAN ABIE ERATO
WEST LIEN STROP

10

CAMP SWAB QUACK
OLEO TILL UNCLE
WORKINGVACATION
LEVER GAIL ADDS
REAL SAWN
ASPS NEVERAGAIN
STU AIRY ALLUDE
CAPON SIC SEDER
ARABIC NOAH RAF
PRETTYUGLY SASS
RAGS LEFT
ESAU NUDE ORATE
NONDAIRYCREAMER
DATED ENTO IMAN
SPIRE REST TOME

11

S	I	N	S		H	E	R	D		M	A	S	T	S
T	M	E	N		E	R	I	E		E	X	T	R	A
R	A	T	E		W	I	L	T		A	L	A	I	N
A	R	T	L	I	N	K	L	E	T	T	E	R		
F	E	L	L	S				S	H	Y		W	I	Z
E	T	E		R	O	T	A	T	E		C	A	R	E
			P	A	L	E	R		S	C	A	R	E	D
		F	R	E	D	C	O	U	P	L	E	S		
S	T	E	A	L	S		O	R	I	O	N			
A	I	R	Y		T	A	M	E	S	T		C	A	M
L	E	O		Q	E	D				H	E	A	V	E
		C	H	A	R	L	I	E	J	O	I	N	E	R
I	D	I	O	T		I	D	L	E		G	A	N	G
M	I	T	L	A		B	E	A	R		E	D	G	E
P	A	Y	E	R		S	A	N	K		R	A	E	S

12

H	A	V	E			U	S	E	S		S	A	G	A
I	M	A	G	E		P	O	G	O		A	M	O	S
S	I	N	G	L	E	S	B	A	R		T	E	R	N
	R	E	S	A	L	E		D	E	R	A	N	G	E
				L	I	T				E	N	D	E	R
U	R	S	A		E	S	C	A	R	P				
N	I	O	B	E			A	R	O	U	S	E	S	
D	O	U	B	L	E	O	R	N	O	T	H	I	N	G
	T	R	E	M	B	L	E			E	E	R	I	E
				O	B	E	Y	E	D		D	E	P	T
A	A	R	O	N				L	O	A				
G	R	U	N	T	E	D		A	L	L	O	U	T	
L	U	M	S		T	R	I	P	L	E	P	L	A	Y
O	B	O	E		N	O	D	S		C	A	N	O	E
W	A	R	T		A	P	S	E			L	A	S	T

13

♥	I	E	R		G	R	A	B		W	A	R	M	♥
S	T	A	Y		R	E	A	R		A	R	E	A	L
H	E	R	E		E	C	R	U		S	T	A	R	E
A	R	A		S	T	E		C	A	P		L	T	S
P	A	C		T	A	N	D	E	M	S		T	I	S
E	T	H	E	R		T	I	L	E		F	O	A	L
D	E	E	M	E	D		S	E	N		O	R	L	Y
			O	P	E	N	♥	E	D	L	Y			
B	R	A	T		T	O	E		S	I	E	G	E	S
R	A	R	E		E	T	N	A		A	R	E	N	A
O	V	A		D	R	E	S	S	E	R		N	S	C
K	E	N		E	S	P		P	A	S		O	U	R
E	L	T	O	N		A	P	E	S		S	E	R	E
N	E	X	U	S		D	I	C	E		U	S	E	D
♥	R	A	T	E		S	E	T	S		R	E	D	♥

14

	C	A	R	E	T			S	T	R	A	T	A	
S	A	V	A	L	A	S		T	E	A	B	A	L	L
T	R	I	N	K	E	T		E	N	T	E	B	B	E
A	D	A	G	E		A	L	A		A	T	B	A	T
R	I	T	E		H	B	O	M	B		S	I	N	O
T	A	O		M	A	L	A	Y	A	N		E	I	N
S	C	R	E	A	M	E	D		B	A	L	S	A	
			S	T	I	R		B	Y	T	E			
	T	V	S	E	T		N	E	S	T	E	G	G	S
F	H	A		D	U	N	A	W	A	Y		A	R	T
R	I	N	D		P	U	T	I	T		A	G	A	R
U	N	I	O	N		G	O	T		P	U	R	S	E
M	A	L	T	O	S	E		C	H	I	N	U	P	S
P	I	L	E	S	I	N		H	U	S	T	L	E	S
	R	A	R	E	S	T			B	A	S	E	D	

15

L	I	S	P			P	A	T	S		A	B	C	S
O	D	O	R	S		A	L	O	T		S	L	U	E
B	L	U	E	C	O	L	L	A	R		T	U	R	N
	E	L	M	E	R			D	E	A	R	E	S	T
			I	N	I	T			S	N	I	P	E	
F	I	B	S	T	E	R		A	S	I	D	E		
O	G	L	E		N	I	P	S		L	E	N	D	S
L	O	U			T	O	R	S	O			C	O	E
D	R	E	G	S		D	O	E	R		S	I	R	E
		B	R	I	B	E		T	A	M	A	L	E	S
	B	O	O	Z	E			S	T	A	N			
S	I	N	C	E	R	E			O	R	D	E	R	
A	N	N	E		B	L	U	E	R	I	B	B	O	N
D	E	E	R		E	L	S	E		A	A	R	O	N
A	T	T	Y		R	E	E	L			R	O	M	E

16

A	W	E	D		I	N	C	U	R		G	L	E	N
C	A	L	I		G	O	O	S	E		L	E	V	I
T	H	E	S	O	U	N	D	O	F	M	U	S	I	C
	L	E	A	D	A					A	I	S	L	E
			B	I	N	D		A	M	I	N			
B	E	L	L	S	A	R	E	R	I	N	G	I	N	G
A	D	I	E	T		E	A	R	L			M	I	R
S	I	N	S		D	A	T	E	D		R	E	N	I
I	C	E			I	M	U	S		S	E	T	O	N
S	T	R	I	K	E	U	P	T	H	E	B	A	N	D
			L	I	S	P		S	O	R	E			
B	R	A	I	N					O	I	L	E	D	
L	A	C	A	G	E	A	U	X	F	O	L	L	E	S
O	V	I	D		G	E	N	I	I		E	M	M	Y
W	E	D	S		G	R	I	S	T		D	O	I	N

17

A	C	T	I		B	L	E	D		T	H	R	O	W
L	O	R	N		R	O	A	D		H	O	O	C	H
F	O	O	T	L	O	O	S	E		W	R	O	T	E
A	L	P	H	O	N	S	E		G	A	S	T	O	N
			E	T	T	E		T	O	R	E			
G	O	P		T	E	N	F	O	O	T	P	O	L	E
C	R	A	N	E			A	N	D		L	U	I	S
L	O	R	E		M	A	T	E	S		A	T	N	O
E	N	D	S		A	M	S			S	Y	R	U	P
F	O	O	T	I	N	M	O	U	T	H		E	S	S
			L	M	N	O		N	E	A	T			
T	O	B	I	A	S		L	E	A	D	O	F	F	S
A	M	O	N	G		P	U	S	S	Y	F	O	O	T
L	A	N	G	E		P	A	C	E		F	A	R	O
C	R	A	S	S		D	U	O	S		S	L	A	P

18

A	R	O	M	A		F	L	E	W		A	P	E	D
M	E	S	A	S		I	O	N	A		L	I	M	E
P	A	S	T	P	E	R	F	O	R	M	A	N	C	E
S	P	A	S		M	E	T	S		A	M	E	E	R
				S	I	D			S	H	O	R	E	
B	A	L	L	E	T		I	O	T	A				
A	L	I	E	N		I	N	K	E	R		E	M	S
I	S	N	O	T	A	G	U	A	R	A	N	T	E	E
L	O	T		I	V	O	R	Y		N	O	R	M	A
				M	O	R	E		M	E	T	E	O	R
	S	I	N	E	W			F	O	E				
C	A	N	O	N		A	L	A	D		L	I	E	U
O	F	F	U	T	U	R	E	R	E	S	U	L	T	S
T	E	E	N		S	I	A	M		I	R	E	N	E
E	R	R	S		O	A	R	S		T	E	X	A	S

19

	C	R	A	F	T			F	A	N	T	A	N	
	E	A	G	L	E	D		A	L	E	R	T	E	D
	S	T	E	E	L	E		S	T	E	A	L	E	R
S	T	I	R	S		P	E	T	E	R		A	D	E
H	M	O		H	A	L	T	E	R		A	N	I	S
E	O	N	S		C	O	E	D		A	N	T	E	S
W	I	S	E	G	U	Y	S		R	O	T	A	R	Y
			R	A	T	S		L	O	N	I			
A	E	R	A	T	E		B	E	D	E	C	K	E	D
G	R	A	P	E		F	A	T	E		S	N	E	E
H	A	T	E		W	O	N	T	O	N		I	R	A
A	S	A		P	A	R	S	E		A	S	T	I	N
S	E	T	T	I	N	G		R	E	B	A	T	E	
T	R	A	I	N	E	E		S	P	O	D	E	S	
	S	T	E	E	D	S			A	B	O	R	T	

20

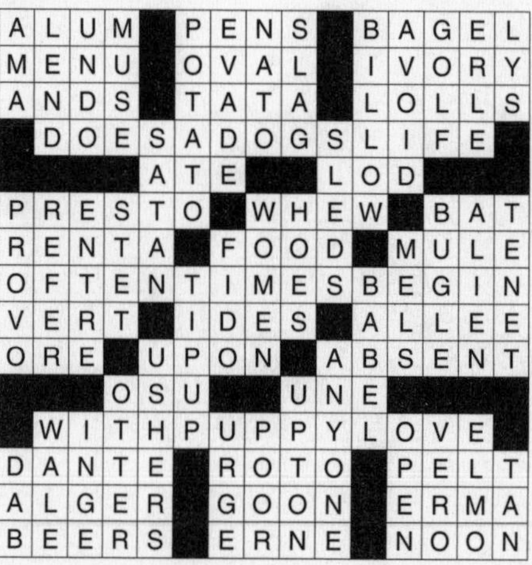

A	L	U	M		P	E	N	S		B	A	G	E	L
M	E	N	U		O	V	A	L		I	V	O	R	Y
A	N	D	S		T	A	T	A		L	O	L	L	S
	D	O	E	S	A	D	O	G	S	L	I	F	E	
				A	T	E			L	O	D			
P	R	E	S	T	O		W	H	E	W		B	A	T
R	E	N	T	A		F	O	O	D		M	U	L	E
O	F	T	E	N	T	I	M	E	S	B	E	G	I	N
V	E	R	T		I	D	E	S		A	L	L	E	E
O	R	E		U	P	O	N		A	B	S	E	N	T
			O	S	U			U	N	E				
	W	I	T	H	P	U	P	P	Y	L	O	V	E	
D	A	N	T	E		R	O	T	O		P	E	L	T
A	L	G	E	R		G	O	O	N		E	R	M	A
B	E	E	R	S		E	R	N	E		N	O	O	N

21

L	A	P	S	E		M	C	S			S	A	T	E
E	L	I	H	U		A	R	P		M	E	R	R	Y
S	E	L	I	G		G	U	A	R	A	N	T	E	E
	G	E	N	E	R	I	C		I	R	I	S	E	S
			G	N	U		I	M	A	G	O			
S	T	A	L	E	R		V	O	T	A	R	I	E	S
T	O	L	E	T		C	E	D	A	R		C	A	N
E	N	O	R	M		O	R	E		E	L	A	T	E
A	T	O		A	R	A	B	S		T	I	M	E	R
M	O	N	A	L	I	S	A		O	F	F	E	N	D
			Y	E	N	T	L		N	A	E			
A	S	S	E	S	S		I	N	E	R	T	I	A	
S	P	E	A	K	E	A	S	Y		R	I	D	G	E
T	A	N	Y	A		D	T	S		A	M	E	E	R
A	N	T	E			E	S	E		R	E	A	D	S

22

		C	O	R	K	S			R	A	V	A	G	E
	R	A	V	I	N	E		R	E	L	I	V	E	S
B	E	N	E	F	I	T		E	X	I	G	E	N	T
A	M	A	R	E	T	T	O	S		T	O	R	T	E
L	A	S	T			E	M	I	L		R	A	L	E
L	I	T	U	P		R	A	D	A	R		G	E	M
S	N	A	R	E	S		N	E	G	A	T	E	S	
			E	A	T	S		D	O	P	E			
	L	E	S	S	E	N	S		S	I	L	I	C	A
M	E	X		E	P	I	C	S		D	E	M	O	N
A	G	E	D		S	P	A	T			S	P	A	N
R	U	M	O	R		P	R	O	S	E	C	U	T	E
I	M	P	L	O	D	E		D	E	V	O	T	E	E
N	E	T	C	O	R	D		G	R	I	P	E	D	
A	S	S	E	T	S			E	E	L	E	D		

23

B	A	L	D		H	A	R	T	E		C	O	S	T
I	L	A	Y		O	N	E	R	S		L	U	K	E
D	O	W	N	A	N	D	O	U	T		O	T	I	S
S	E	N	A	T	O	R	S		A	L	S	O	P	S
			M	I	R	E		S	T	E	E	N		
O	T	O	O	L	E		C	H	E	E	T	A	H	S
L	O	U		T	E	R	R	A		S	E	L	A	H
M	O	T	S		S	E	E	M	S		D	I	N	O
A	N	T	I	C		L	E	E	K	S		M	O	O
N	E	O	N	A	T	E	S		I	N	A	B	I	T
		L	I	G	H	T		S	L	I	D			
A	B	U	S	E	R		S	H	I	P	M	A	T	E
W	A	N	T		O	U	T	O	F	S	I	G	H	T
O	N	C	E		B	L	U	E	T		T	R	E	E
L	E	H	R		S	E	N	D	S		S	A	Y	S

24

S	H	E	D	S		B	O	G	Y		O	P	E	N
P	I	X	I	E		E	G	O	S		P	I	L	E
A	V	A	N	T	G	A	R	D	E		T	E	L	E
R	E	M		T	R	U	E		R	A	I	D	E	D
			E	L	I	X	I	R		M	O	A	N	S
F	A	B	L	E	D		S	E	C	A	N	T		
O	B	I	S			A	H	W	A	Z		E	R	A
A	B	L	A	T	E	S		E	Y	E	B	R	O	W
M	E	L		R	A	T	E	D			A	R	A	L
		E	D	I	T	E	D		S	A	Y	E	R	S
A	N	T	I	C		R	U	M	P	U	S			
D	O	D	G	E	S		C	O	A	T		D	A	B
O	B	O	E		P	L	A	T	D	U	J	O	U	R
P	L	U	S		O	A	T	H		M	A	L	T	A
T	E	X	T		T	Y	E	S		N	Y	L	O	N

25

D	O	M	E	S		M	A	S	K			U	M	P
A	L	I	V	E		A	L	I	E		A	P	E	R
Y	I	N	A	N	D	Y	A	N	G		G	A	L	A
S	O	T		A	D	O	R	E	S		A	N	E	W
				T	E	R	M			W	I	D	E	N
L	A	D	L	E		S	E	S	T	I	N	A		
A	L	O	E				D	E	E	R		B	U	N
D	A	W	D	L	E	R		A	N	E	M	O	N	E
S	I	N		O	M	A	R				A	U	T	O
		A	D	A	P	T	E	D		G	E	T	O	N
P	I	N	E	D			N	U	D	E				
R	O	D	E		S	T	E	R	E	O		C	P	A
A	T	O	M		N	O	W	A	N	D	T	H	E	N
T	A	U	S		I	R	A	N		E	V	I	C	T
E	S	T			P	E	L	T		S	A	C	K	S

26

```
R E B E L ■ E G B D F ■ W A G
A R O M A ■ B R O A D ■ E E L
M A X I M ■ B O X C A M E R A
■ ■ O T I S ■ V E E ■ O D I N
A L F ■ A C H E D ■ R A Y E D
D U F F ■ H E L I C E S ■ ■ ■
M A I L B O X ■ N A B ■ S H E
E N C O I L ■ ■ ■ J O S H U A
N N E ■ T A J ■ B O X C A R S
■ ■ ■ P E R U S A L ■ I D L E
O P A L S ■ K H M E R ■ O Y L
R I C E ■ O E R ■ S H A W ■ ■
S Q U A W K B O X ■ E M B E R
O U T ■ I L O V E ■ A B O V E
N E E ■ T A X E S ■ S I X E D
```

27

```
A C A T ■ ■ C A T E R ■ A S S
R A G E S ■ O R A T E ■ M I T
C R U N C H B E R R Y ■ O N E
O P E N A I R ■ P E N A N C E
■ ■ ■ ■ L E A ■ ■ ■ A N G E L
H A R P E R S F E R R Y ■ ■ ■
A L I A S ■ ■ I R E D ■ P O M
R E N D ■ P A L E D ■ J A V A
P E G ■ T I N T ■ ■ S O R E R
■ ■ ■ M A T T H E W P E R R Y
I B E A M ■ ■ ■ C H E ■ ■ ■ ■
N I A G A R A ■ H E N R E I D
L O S ■ L O N D O N D E R R Y
A T E ■ E S T E E ■ S A G A N
W A D ■ S E E M S ■ ■ L O N E
```

28

```
H A L L ■ ■ A L M S ■ S I L O
A R I A S ■ C O A L ■ K N A P
J A M U P J E L L Y T I G H T
I B E R I A ■ L I L I ■ E R S
■ ■ ■ E R M A ■ G Y P ■ ■ ■ ■
J E L L Y B E A N ■ T E V Y E
A N A ■ ■ S O B ■ ■ O C E A N
M O T I F ■ N O N ■ P O R T O
E L E N I ■ ■ V I P ■ ■ D E C
S A X O N ■ J E L L Y F I S H
■ ■ ■ E M U ■ S A U L ■ ■ ■ ■
A D E ■ L A R K ■ S K O A L S
J E L L Y R O L L M O R T O N
A L I T ■ T R E E ■ N A O M I
R E E D ■ A S E A ■ ■ S P A T
```

29

```
T A P ■ A S S U M E ■ D R A B
A V A ■ S H U T I N ■ E A V E
R E P ■ P A P E R H A N G E R
P R E S I D E S ■ A T T E S T
■ ■ R A R E R ■ A N T I ■ ■ ■
E U C L I D ■ B I C U S P I D
A S H E N ■ H I D E ■ T A R O
R E A ■ S H Y N E S S ■ P E N
L U S T ■ O D D S ■ O B E S E
S P E A K E R S ■ E C A R T E
■ ■ ■ R E D O ■ M U R A T ■ ■
A D A G I O ■ L O C A L I Z E
P A P E R W E I G H T ■ G E L
E R S T ■ N A T U R E ■ E R A
S E E S ■ S T E L E S ■ R O N
```

30

```
S C A T ■ L A R D ■ ■ T H I S
R A S H ■ A L O E ■ R O O S T
S T I R ■ W E A R ■ E C O L E
■ O N E E Y E D M O N S T E R
■ ■ ■ S T E ■ ■ ■ D E I S T ■
O N E H O R S E T O W N ■ ■ ■
P A T E N ■ L E E R S ■ R O W
A P A R ■ ■ A L T ■ ■ L A M A
L E S ■ A B N E R ■ S A V E R
■ ■ ■ O N E T R A C K M I N D
■ K O R D A ■ ■ ■ H I E ■ ■ ■
O N E A R M E D B A N D I T ■
G E S T E ■ G O O F ■ U V E A
R E T O W ■ A D Z E ■ C A R R
E D E R ■ ■ D O O R ■ K N I T
```

31

F	L	E	X			S	W	A	P		M	A	A	M
R	O	R	Y		A	C	A	S	E		A	L	D	O
E	L	I	Z	A	B	E	T	H	T	A	Y	L	O	R
T	A	N		L	I	N	T	Y		R	E	I	G	N
			C	E	D	E			S	I	R			
A	P	L	A	C	E	I	N	T	H	E	S	U	N	
T	R	I	P				U	R	A	L		N	O	V
T	Y	N	E		O	P	R	A	H		S	I	N	E
N	O	D		A	C	E	S				H	O	E	R
	R	A	I	N	T	R	E	E	C	O	U	N	T	Y
			B	I	O			A	H	O	T			
O	B	J	E	T		M	A	R	I	N		I	L	L
C	O	U	R	A	G	E	O	F	L	A	S	S	I	E
H	A	D	I		A	N	N	U	L		A	L	F	A
S	T	O	A		D	U	E	L			W	E	E	K

32

W	O	V	E	N		M	A	P	L	E		W	A	D
I	N	A	N	E		A	L	L	A	Y		A	V	A
G	O	L	D	E	N	G	L	O	B	E		Y	O	M
				D	E	U	S			L	E	N	I	N
M	O	D	U	L	E	S		F	E	E	L	E	R	S
E	R	A	S	E	D		T	O	R	S	O	S		
A	B	I	E	S		R	E	A	M	S		W	A	S
N	I	L	S		F	I	R	M	A		B	O	N	A
S	T	Y		B	O	O	R	S		P	O	R	G	Y
		P	E	L	O	T	A		B	I	L	L	I	E
B	A	L	L	O	T	S		B	R	O	O	D	E	R
A	L	A	M	O			S	E	E	N				
K	I	N		M	O	T	H	E	R	E	A	R	T	H
E	V	E		E	L	I	O	T		E	L	I	A	S
S	E	T		R	E	N	T	S		R	E	A	C	T

33

G	L	U	M		A	T	L	A	S		E	L	A	L
L	I	S	A		R	H	E	T	T		R	I	T	A
A	M	E	R	I	C	A	S	F	R	E	E	D	O	M
D	E	D	I	C	A	T	E		I	N	C	O	M	E
			N	E	D	S		S	C	O	T			
P	A	L	A	C	E		S	A	K	S		N	A	B
R	I	A	T	A		S	E	V	E		D	U	M	A
I	N	D	E	P	E	N	D	E	N	C	E	D	A	Y
A	G	E	S		T	E	E	S		O	P	I	N	E
M	E	N		C	H	A	R		S	P	R	E	A	D
			S	H	E	D		P	A	T	E			
E	S	T	H	E	R		P	A	L	I	S	A	D	E
P	Y	R	O	T	E	C	H	N	I	C	S	H	O	W
O	N	E	R		A	R	D	E	N		O	O	Z	E
S	E	E	N		L	I	S	L	E		R	Y	E	S

34

H	U	M	A	N		B	A	T	H		A	B	A	B
A	B	O	L	T		A	R	E	A		S	A	G	E
H	E	R	S	H	E	Y	B	A	R		T	R	U	E
A	R	N	O		G	O	O	S	E		A	B	E	T
				F	O	U	R			T	R	E	S	S
R	A	B	B	I	S		S	P	A	R	E	R		
A	W	A	R	D				U	N	I		S	S	S
P	A	R	A	D	E	S		N	Y	M	P	H	E	T
S	Y	M		L	A	C				M	A	O	R	I
		I	B	E	R	I	A		P	E	P	P	E	R
L	A	T	E	R			R	O	A	D				
L	I	Z	A		S	H	I	N	S		D	O	R	A
A	D	V	T		P	A	S	S	T	H	E	B	A	R
M	E	A	T		A	L	E	E		A	L	I	K	E
A	S	H	Y		R	E	N	T		M	I	T	E	S

35

R	A	Y	E		D	U	P	E		P	L	U	G	S
E	L	E	V		O	R	A	L		R	O	M	E	O
S	T	L	O		W	A	L	L	T	O	W	A	L	L
P	E	L	L	M	E	L	L		I	T	E			
		O	V	A	L	S		S	N	O	R	I	N	G
T	O	W	E	R	S		D	E	S	C		L	E	R
H	U	B	S			C	A	M	E	O		L	E	E
U	T	E		I	L	L	W	I	L	L		O	S	E
M	E	L		M	O	O	N	S			A	G	O	N
B	A	L		M	V	P	S		R	A	C	I	N	E
S	T	Y	M	I	E	S		L	I	L	A	C		
			E	N	L		R	O	L	L	C	A	L	L
V	O	L	L	E	Y	B	A	L	L		I	L	I	A
A	R	I	O	N		A	B	L	E		A	L	O	T
T	R	E	N	T		N	E	S	T		S	Y	N	E

36

A	L	A	S		B	A	N	D	B		G	L	O	B
R	O	M	P		O	W	N	E	R		L	O	N	I
A	L	A	I		L	E	E	I	A	C	O	C	C	A
B	A	S	K	E	T	S			V	A	R	I	E	S
			E	T	S			C	O	S	I			
B	E	L	L	E		S	P	A		T	A	S	S	O
E	R	I	E		H	E	A	R	S	E		A	P	R
R	O	B	E	R	T	E	D	W	A	R	D	L	E	E
E	S	E		A	S	T	R	A	Y		O	S	L	O
T	E	L	L	S		H	E	X		O	R	A	L	S
			E	P	E	E			F	B	I			
C	H	A	F	E	D			A	R	I	S	I	N	G
L	E	E	T	R	E	V	I	N	O		L	O	A	N
A	R	O	O		N	I	K	O	N		E	T	N	A
P	E	N	N		S	P	E	N	T		E	A	S	T

37

R	E	W	E	D		H	U	P		T	A	C	T	S
A	B	O	D	E		U	S	A		A	L	O	H	A
W	O	R	D	G	A	M	E	S		X	A	X	E	S
L	A	D	Y		S	I	R	S		I	M	A	M	S
S	T	S		H	A	D		W	A	C	O			
		Q	T	I	P		W	O	N	A		W	A	S
A	G	U	A	S		W	O	R	D	B	O	O	K	S
L	O	A	M		W	O	R	D	S		B	R	I	G
F	O	R	E	W	O	R	D	S		D	I	D	N	T
A	D	E		A	N	D	Y		P	I	E	S		
			A	C	T	S		C	O	X		W	P	A
S	L	I	N	K		A	J	A	R		M	O	A	N
L	U	N	D	I		L	A	S	T	W	O	R	D	S
A	C	A	R	E		A	V	E		E	N	T	R	E
P	E	T	E	R		D	A	Y		E	T	H	E	L

38

S	A	M	B	A		A	C	N	E		S	W	A	G
A	R	I	E	L		S	H	U	N		O	H	I	O
V	A	N	N	A	W	H	I	T	E		N	I	L	E
E	L	I	S		H	E	N	S		D	A	T	E	S
				R	E	N	E		M	E	T	E	D	
N	E	W	T	O	N		S	E	E	S	A	W		
E	T	H	E	L		B	E	A	S	T		A	D	A
S	T	I	L	L	E	R		C	A	R	O	T	I	D
T	A	T		T	R	A	S	H		U	P	E	N	D
		E	L	O	I	S	E		S	C	A	R	E	S
	S	H	A	P	E		A	B	E	T				
S	L	O	P	S		A	W	O	L		S	L	I	T
P	I	U	S		P	E	A	R	L	W	H	I	T	E
E	L	S	E		E	R	L	E		R	O	L	E	X
D	Y	E	D		G	O	L	D		Y	E	A	S	T

39

(T)	H	A	D		B	A	T	S		S	O	C	K	O
A	(A)	R	E		O	L	I	N		A	S	H	E	N
I	L	(K)	S		R	I	C	O		Y	E	A	R	S
L	O	S	(E)	O	N	E	S	W	A	Y		I	R	E
				(T)	E	N		G	I	E		R	S	T
I	N	T	O	T	(O)		M	O	R	S	E	L		
H	O	R	N	E		(T)	A	O	S		B	I	N	D
A	D	A	I	R		O	(H)	S		A	S	F	O	R
D	E	V	O		L	U	R	(E)		B	E	T	T	E
		E	N	T	I	C	E		(S)	E	N	S	E	D
G	A	R		O	O	H		A	W	(L)				
O	P	S		U	N	D	E	V	E	L	(O)	P	E	D
T	R	I	P	P		O	B	O	E		S	(P)	R	Y
T	I	N	G	E		W	R	I	T		S	P	(E)	E
A	L	G	A	E		N	O	D	S		A	S	I	(S)

40

M	O	S	S		A	T	R	I	P		C	A	R	P
A	T	T	U		M	A	U	N	A		O	B	O	E
S	T	U	B	B	O	R	N	A	S	A	M	U	L	E
C	O	N	S	O	R	T	S		T	E	E	T	E	R
			C	P	A	S		D	I	O	R			
L	A	U	R	E	L		L	I	M	N		O	A	S
A	R	T	I	E		G	A	V	E		I	N	T	O
S	L	I	P	P	E	R	Y	A	S	A	N	E	E	L
S	E	C	T		D	A	I	S		R	A	I	S	E
O	N	A		R	E	I	N		S	T	U	N	T	S
			P	E	N	N		M	A	I	D			
A	S	S	E	N	T		C	A	L	L	I	S	T	O
N	A	K	E	D	A	S	A	J	A	Y	B	I	R	D
O	B	I	T		T	U	T	O	R		L	A	I	R
N	U	D	E		E	M	O	R	Y		E	M	M	A

41

R	E	D	P	E	P	P	E	R		A	P	H	I	D
I	R	R	A	D	I	A	T	E		G	R	E	C	O
C	H	A	R	G	E	D	A	F	F	A	I	R	E	S
H	A	W	S	E	R				L	I	M	I	T	
E	R	L	E			S	I	M	O	N		T	O	W
R	D	S		S	E	E	S	A	W		L	A	N	A
			B	A	R	T	O	K		S	O	G	G	Y
	B	E	L	L	E	S	L	E	T	T	R	E	S	
T	R	Y	I	T		H	A	W	A	I	I			
S	E	E	P		H	O	T	A	I	R		C	P	O
P	A	P		L	A	T	E	R			G	A	R	R
	T	I	T	U	S				D	A	R	R	I	N
C	H	E	R	C	H	E	Z	L	A	F	E	M	M	E
D	E	C	O	R		G	O	O	N	A	T	E	A	R
C	R	E	T	E		G	E	N	E	R	A	L	L	Y

42

O	S	L	O		P	A	T	E	S		S	T	A	G
F	L	A	P		A	W	A	K	E		L	O	L	A
F	I	V	E	S	T	A	R	G	E	N	E	R	A	L
S	T	A	R	T	E	R	S		D	E	P	O	N	E
			A	R	N	E		P	I	C	T			
C	A	S	T	E	S		L	E	E	K		T	E	T
E	T	H	O	S		O	A	R	S		P	E	R	E
S	T	A	R	S	A	N	D	S	T	R	I	P	E	S
T	A	N	S		I	S	E	E		E	L	E	C	T
A	R	K		B	R	E	D		A	S	S	E	T	S
			M	O	L	T		F	L	E	E			
T	I	V	O	L	I		S	A	T	A	N	I	S	T
S	T	A	R	O	F	B	E	T	H	L	E	H	E	M
A	S	I	S		T	E	A	S	E		R	O	T	E
R	A	L	E		S	A	M	O	A		S	P	A	N

43

A	S	T	A		T	E	R	N		O	P	A	R	T
M	E	A	L		K	N	E	E		V	I	R	E	O
P	A	P	A	D	O	C	D	U	V	A	L	I	E	R
S	T	E	R	E		H	O	R	A		S	A	F	E
			M	Y	R	A		A	L	A	N			
S	O	B	S		U	N	C	L	E	R	E	M	U	S
A	T	E		M	E	T	H		T	I	R	A	N	A
M	A	G	D	A		S	I	P		E	S	S	A	Y
O	R	I	E	N	T		N	A	G	S		O	P	S
A	U	N	T	I	E	M	A	M	E		U	N	T	O
			H	A	L	O		P	L	A	T			
A	G	A	R		I	D	E	E		R	A	N	T	O
D	R	J	O	Y	C	E	B	R	O	T	H	E	R	S
D	I	A	N	A		M	R	E	D		A	N	I	L
S	T	R	E	P		S	O	R	E		N	E	M	O

44

H	A	R	P	S		A	B	E	E		M	E	A	D
A	D	I	E	U		C	E	L	T		I	S	L	E
H	O	T	O	N	T	H	E	H	E	E	L	S	O	F
A	G	E	N	D	A		B	I	R	D	D	O	G	
			A	D	E			N	E	E				
H	E	R	H	E	A	R	T	W	A	S	W	A	R	M
A	R	O	O			R	O	I	L	S		C	I	A
V	A	M	P	S		A	N	S		A	G	E	N	T
O	T	E		T	O	T	I	E			E	R	S	E
C	O	O	L	A	S	A	C	U	C	U	M	B	E	R
			A	T	H			P	U	N				
	S	T	R	I	K	E	S		B	I	A	F	R	A
P	O	U	R	C	O	L	D	W	A	T	E	R	O	N
A	I	N	U		S	L	A	Y		E	R	E	C	T
S	L	A	P		H	A	K	E		S	O	D	A	S

45

M	E	L	E	E		F	A	C	T		T	A	S	K
A	C	A	S	E		A	M	O	R		A	R	L	O
T	H	I	C	K	J	U	I	C	Y	S	T	E	A	K
H	O	R	A		U	N	D	O		H	A	S	T	O
			P	A	D				K	I	M			
F	R	I	E	D	O	N	I	O	N	R	I	N	G	S
R	A	T	E	S		A	S	H	O	T		A	H	A
A	N	T	S		B	F	L	A	T		G	I	A	N
N	C	O		C	A	T	E	R		M	E	A	N	T
C	H	O	C	O	L	A	T	E	S	U	N	D	A	E
			A	M	I				E	G	O			
S	H	A	R	I		F	I	J	I		V	A	N	E
H	I	G	H	C	H	O	L	E	S	T	E	R	O	L
O	R	E	O		E	X	I	T		U	S	E	R	S
W	E	E	P		N	Y	E	T		B	E	A	M	E

46

A	S	P	E	N		D	A	L	I		A	M	I	D
T	H	E	S	E		E	G	A	N		V	I	V	A
T	A	S	T	E		M	O	T	S		E	L	A	N
	G	O	O	D	N	I	G	H	T	I	R	E	N	E
			P	L	O			S	E	C				
P	A	R		E	L	K	E		P	I	E	C	E	S
O	R	A	L		A	I	L	S		E	R	O	D	E
L	O	V	E	A	N	D	M	A	R	R	I	A	G	E
E	M	E	N	D		S	E	M	I		S	T	E	M
S	A	N	D	A	L		R	E	S	T		I	R	S
				G	A	L			E	O	N			
I	L	L	B	E	S	E	E	I	N	G	Y	O	U	
N	E	A	R		T	E	R	N		G	L	A	R	E
K	A	T	E		E	R	I	N		L	O	R	D	S
S	K	E	W		D	Y	E	S		E	N	S	U	E

47

C	O	R	M		I	N	C	A		S	C	R	A	P
O	L	I	O		M	E	L	D		A	H	O	M	E
M	E	N	U		P	A	I	L		S	I	M	O	N
M	I	S	S	M	A	R	M	E	L	S	T	E	I	N
A	C	E	T	I	C		B	R	A	E				
			A	T	T	U			T	R	E	B	L	E
E	V	I	C	T		N	A	P	E		T	R	O	Y
W	I	S	H	Y	O	U	W	E	R	E	H	E	R	E
E	L	I	E		L	M	N	O		L	O	W	E	R
S	E	N	S	E	D			N	O	E	L			
				L	I	S	P		S	N	O	R	E	S
W	H	E	N	W	E	M	E	E	T	A	G	A	I	N
R	O	M	E	O		E	T	T	E		I	N	D	O
A	M	I	N	O		W	A	R	N		S	T	E	R
P	O	L	E	D		S	L	E	D		T	O	R	T

48

D	O	R	M		S	E	D	E	R		S	A	M	P
A	S	T	I		H	A	U	T	E		T	R	I	O
T	H	E	S	P	O	R	T	O	F	K	I	N	G	S
E	A	S	T	E	R	L	Y		A	R	R	E	S	T
			R	A	T	S		A	S	I	S			
N	A	D	I	R	S		P	E	T	S		S	T	A
I	D	E	A	L		P	A	R	E		O	N	E	R
D	A	I	L	Y	R	A	C	I	N	G	F	O	R	M
E	G	G	S		E	P	E	E		A	F	O	R	E
S	E	N		S	C	A	R		M	I	S	T	E	D
			A	I	R	S		R	I	T	E			
S	T	A	P	L	E		R	E	L	E	A	S	E	S
W	I	N	P	L	A	C	E	A	N	D	S	H	O	W
A	L	T	A		T	R	A	D	E		O	O	N	A
P	E	E	L		E	I	D	E	R		N	O	S	Y

49

S	E	M	I		G	A	L	A	S		A	F	A	R
I	R	A	Q		A	L	I	C	E		L	U	L	U
F	I	R	S	T	O	F	T	H	E	M	O	N	T	H
T	E	E		A	L	I	S			I	N	T	E	R
			F	L	E	E		P	I	N	E			
C	A	L	L	E	R		S	E	A	N		S	F	C
A	L	O	E			C	O	N	G	O		P	E	R
M	I	D	D	L	E	O	F	N	O	W	H	E	R	E
E	G	G		A	R	R	A	Y			Y	A	M	S
O	N	E		Y	I	P	S		E	S	P	R	I	T
			S	O	N	S		L	U	C	E			
W	O	O	L	F			T	O	G	A		P	I	T
E	N	D	O	F	T	H	E	C	E	N	T	U	R	Y
S	T	O	P		R	O	M	A	N		A	M	O	R
T	O	R	E		A	P	P	L	E		M	A	N	E

50

A	L	G	A		I	D	E	A			T	A	R	P
S	E	E	D		S	E	W	U	P		E	L	I	A
C	A	R	O	L	I	N	E	K	E	N	N	E	D	Y
A	G	A		U	S	E			G	O	O	S	E	S
P	U	L	L	S		B	O	L	G	E	R			
	E	D	I	T	H		R	A	Y	S		L	E	E
		F	O	R	A		I	N	C		F	E	E	L
L	E	O	N	A	R	D	O	D	A	V	I	N	C	I
E	R	R	S		P	A	L		S	I	N	N		
X	E	D		A	O	N	E		S	L	A	Y	S	
			E	N	M	E	S	H		E	L	B	O	W
M	T	E	T	N	A			E	S	L		R	U	E
R	I	C	H	A	R	D	D	R	E	Y	F	U	S	S
E	T	R	E		X	E	R	O	X		I	C	E	T
D	O	U	R			B	U	S	Y		T	E	D	S

51

B	A	H	S			E	N	O	S			T	H	Y
A	L	E	E		A	R	E	N	A		W	H	E	E
J	O	L	L	Y	G	R	E	E	N	G	I	A	N	T
A	P	P	E	A	R	S				O	R	R	S	
			N	R	A			D	I	N	E	D		
G	R	E	E	N	I	N	J	U	D	G	M	E	N	T
R	E	X			N	E	A	R	S		A	S	I	A
E	A	C	H			A	S	H			N	E	X	T
A	C	H	E		S	T	O	A	T			R	I	A
T	H	E	G	R	E	E	N	M	O	N	S	T	E	R
		Q	U	I	N	N			L	E	T			
	F	U	M	E				S	E	R	I	A	L	S
G	R	E	E	N	B	A	C	K	D	O	L	L	A	R
E	A	R	N		M	A	R	I	O		L	I	S	A
D	T	S			W	H	I	T			S	E	T	S

52

M	A	R	I	A		C	A	R	A	T		C	A	Y
A	L	O	N	G		O	S	A	G	E		A	D	O
T	O	M	T	E	R	R	I	F	I	C		T	R	U
C	H	A	R		Y	E	S		T	H	E	B	A	R
H	A	N	O	V	E	R		R	A	I	L	A	G	E
				A	S	S		S	T	E	A	L		
T	I	K	I	S			A	V	E		I	L	I	E
O	V	I	N	E		L	I	P		A	N	O	D	E
W	E	T	S		M	A	R			R	E	U	S	E
		T	O	T	E	D		S	A	M				
P	A	Y	L	O	A	D		A	N	S	W	E	R	S
O	C	H	E	R	S		A	W	E		A	L	O	E
P	T	A		P	U	S	S	Y	W	I	L	L	O	W
P	O	W		O	R	A	T	E		A	L	E	N	E
A	R	K		R	E	T	A	R		M	A	N	E	D

53

		P	A	R	S	E		P	E	A	R	S		
C	R	A	N	I	U	M		A	E	S	O	P	S	
R	E	R	A	T	E	S		C	R	E	M	A	T	E
A	D	E	L	E			R	E	O		A	R	A	P
S	O	S	O		P	L	E	D		S	I	E	N	A
			G	A	L	E	N		R	A	N			
I	M	A		V	A	N	E		E	L	E	V	E	N
L	A	W		A	N	A	G	R	A	M		I	W	O
K	I	N	D	L	E		A	E	R	O		M	E	G
			R	O	T		D	A	M	N	S			
C	H	A	I	N		D	E	M	S		C	R	O	P
L	O	P	E		S	I	S			P	R	A	D	O
U	S	E	D	C	A	R		S	T	R	I	P	E	D
	T	R	U	D	G	E		I	S	O	M	E	R	S
		S	P	E	A	R		R	E	A	P	S		

54

C	L	O	B	B	E	R		S	A	L		F	L	O
D	E	S	E	R	V	E		C	R	A	T	I	O	N
S	A	L	L	I	E	D		I	M	P	A	S	S	E
	P	O	L	A	R	O	P	P	O	S	I	T	E	S
			E	N	S		E	I	R	E				
M	A	G	S			E	G	O			M	O	N	A
A	P	R		E	A	R	L		M	A	D	D	O	G
C	H	I	L	L	Y	R	E	C	E	P	T	I	O	N
H	I	P	P	I	E		G	A	L	E		U	N	E
O	D	E	S			M	G	M			A	M	E	S
				W	H	E	E		I	A	N			
C	O	O	L	H	E	A	D	E	D	N	E	S	S	
O	N	G	O	I	N	G		R	E	D	M	E	A	T
K	I	R	S	T	I	E		L	A	R	I	A	T	S
E	N	E		E	E	R		E	L	E	C	T	E	E

55

U	S	A	F		C	A	S	T			A	B	B	A
H	A	R	I		R	I	P	U	P		P	L	O	Y
F	A	T	S	D	O	M	I	N	O		R	A	G	E
	R	I	C	O			K	I	T	H		C	I	A
		C	H	U	B	B	Y	C	H	E	C	K	E	R
	T	H	E	B	A	Y		S	E	R	A			
C	H	O	R	T	L	E	D		R	E	M	O	V	E
O	A	K				S	O	D				R	A	T
D	R	E	A	M	T		C	A	L	A	B	A	S	H
			Y	U	R	I		M	A	L	O	N	E	
S	K	I	N	N	Y	D	I	P	P	I	N	G		
H	E	R		I	S	A	R			B	A	E	R	
O	N	E	S		T	H	E	T	H	I	N	M	A	N
C	Y	S	T		S	O	N	A	R		Z	E	R	O
K	A	T	E			S	E	N	S		A	N	E	W

56

MAGUS■HEMP■BASS
OCALA■ALAI■ARIA
THENUDISTCOLONY
■ELATED■TAR■LAS
■■■SET■SERAGLIO
ELF■DOOM■DNA■■■
RARE■URIS■GLOB■
GROVERCLEVELAND
■AMEN■HITE■OKAY
■■■RAF■NERO■SIE
IMCOMING■IDA■■■
OAR■EGO■STELLA■
THEBLARNEYSTONE
AREA■RACE■SOLTI
SEPT■ODOR■ANAIS

57

DEBRA■PLACE■ABE
ARLES■CONAN■RED
FRENCHTOAST■ENG
NESTEA■STARGAZE
EDS■TLC■■BAA■■■
■■■■ITALIANHERO
JAM■CELEB■TAKER
OPAL■RIVET■NEAL
GOTUP■PERIL■DRY
SPANISHRICE■■■■
■■■ACT■■ATE■QBS
DISRAELI■ACTUAL
ROT■SWISSCHEESE
ANY■SETTO■ELLIE
WAX■ODEON■RELET

58

■MEHTA■■GASLAMP
MAYORS■TALLULAH
ANEMIA■OBLIGATE
RECAP■SNEAD■NEW
■■AGEING■YET■■■
RATE■DAUBS■AJAR
UPC■LEPER■RIATA
MPH■CASTOFF■WIN
PLEAD■OWNED■BLT
SERB■ONICE■ARTS
■■■COG■SOLACE■■
ASK■FLATS■SCARS
DOESTIME■KOOKIE
DARKENER■INSECT
SPRINGS■■METRO■

59

BASEL■AMIS■BALS
ADALE■RANT■IMON
TEXAS■ANDA■SODA
ELOPER■AIRSTRIP
DENS■ONTARIO■■■
■■■ERNIE■■DUAL■
MVP■ANTE■DERMIS
GEORGIA■NEWYORK
SECEDE■SOFA■SAY
■ROTO■■TREYS■■■
■■■ALABAMA■ASEA
SPOILERS■TENETS
PENN■SASE■IDAHO
RACE■OVER■NOTON
YSER■PONE■EROSE

60

■CASTANET■LIFT■
DALAILAMA■EGRET
ANTIPASTO■AGILE
UTE■SPA■■PRICER
BORSTAL■PENNAME
■■■LES■CARESSES
■SAAR■POLED■STA
MARY■CARES■TEES
INT■POPES■PIER■
STIMULUS■DIN■■■
LACONIA■PRESIDE
ECHOIC■■HOR■GOV
AROSE■PROVOLONE
DUKES■ABNEGATES
■ZEST■DIESIRAE■

61

A	B	C	S		C	A	R	U	S	O		J	A	R
R	I	L	L		O	P	E	N	E	D		U	M	A
C	L	A	U	D	E	R	A	I	N	S		D	A	M
S	K	Y	G	O	D		P	T	A		A	D	Z	E
				L	I	S		S	T	E	P	H	E	N
U	N	J	I	L	T	E	D		E	L	O	I		
R	O	A	N		O	W	E	N		O	G	R	E	S
S	E	C	T		R	E	M	I	T		E	S	S	O
A	S	K	E	W		R	O	N	A		E	C	T	O
		L	A	I	C		B	A	N	K	S	H	O	T
E	M	E	R	G	E	S		S	K	A				
L	A	M	S		T	O	E		A	S	I	A	N	S
I	S	M		J	E	F	F	B	R	I	D	G	E	S
Z	O	O		O	R	A	T	E	D		O	U	S	T
A	N	N		B	A	S	S	E	S		L	E	S	S

62

L	A	S	H		E	D	G	A	R		B	R	A	T
A	S	K	A		S	A	R	T	O		R	O	T	H
W	H	A	T	S	T	H	A	T	Y	O	U	S	A	Y
N	O	T	R	E			D	I	A	R	I	S	T	
S	W	E	A	R	A	T		C	L	A	S	P		
			C	A	R	A	T			T	E	E	N	S
P	E	C	K		O	L	I	O		O	R	R	I	N
E	T	O		I	W	O	N	D	E	R		O	K	A
S	T	U	D	S		N	E	E	D		S	T	E	P
T	U	N	I	S			D	U	N	C	E			
		S	M	U	T	S		M	A	H	A	L	I	A
	R	E	P	E	A	T	S			I	C	O	N	S
W	E	L	L	S	H	U	T	M	Y	M	O	U	T	H
O	B	O	E		O	R	E	A	D		W	I	R	E
W	A	R	D		E	M	M	Y	S		S	E	A	N

63

G	A	L	A	S		F	U	M		J	O	K	E	R
A	L	E	U	T		I	T	O		O	V	I	N	E
M	E	A	N	Y		F	A	D		T	E	T	O	N
Y	E	R	T	L	E	T	H	E	T	U	R	T	L	E
			I	O	N	E		M	I	N	H			
L	U	B	E		D	E	R		T	H	E	O	N	E
A	N	O		H	O	N	E	D		E	A	S	E	L
I	F	I	R	A	N	T	H	E	C	I	R	C	U	S
R	E	S	O	W		H	A	R	U	M		A	R	A
S	D	E	A	T	H		B	I	T		E	R	O	S
			S	H	A	G		V	E	A	L			
H	O	R	T	O	N	H	E	A	R	S	A	W	H	O
A	C	T	E	R		O	R	B		T	I	E	U	P
S	T	E	R	N		S	I	L		A	N	D	R	E
P	O	S	S	E		T	E	E		R	E	S	T	S

64

W	A	R	P	A	T	H		U	P	S	C	A	L	E
E	L	E	C	T	E	E		G	E	O	R	G	I	A
S	A	N	T	A	N	A		L	A	W	Y	E	R	S
T	N	T			E	D	D	Y		E	S	S	A	Y
			B	Y	T	H	E		A	R	T			
M	E	L	E	E		U	M	P	S		A	B	E	L
E	X	A	L	T		N	O	A	H		L	O	L	A
C	E	L	L	I	S	T		G	E	T	B	U	S	Y
C	R	A	B		P	E	T	E		R	A	T	I	O
A	T	W	O		A	R	A	T		O	L	S	E	N
			T	I	M		P	U	P	I	L			
S	C	O	T	S		V	E	R	A			I	R	A
H	E	R	O	I	N	E		N	I	C	E	G	U	Y
A	D	A	M	A	N	T		E	N	C	L	O	S	E
W	E	L	S	H	E	S		R	E	C	I	T	E	S

65

S	T	R	O	P		S	P	A		S	M	A	S	H
C	I	A	N	O		A	I	D		L	I	M	P	Y
O	T	T	E	R		L	E	D		A	X	I	O	M
W	H	O	L	E	W	A	T	E	R	M	E	L	O	N
L	E	N	O		A	Z	A	N	A		D	E	N	S
			I	O	N	A		D	I	N	G			
S	P	E	N	C	E	R		A	D	O	R	N	E	D
C	U	L	P	A						R	E	U	S	E
I	N	S	O	L	E	S		A	S	S	E	N	T	S
			R	A	N	T		S	T	E	N			
O	I	N	K		C	A	S	T	E		S	A	P	S
C	H	I	C	K	E	N	T	A	R	R	A	G	O	N
T	O	T	H	E		D	O	R		A	L	I	N	E
A	P	R	O	N		E	A	T		V	A	N	C	E
D	E	E	P	S		E	T	E		E	D	G	E	R

66

A	M	A	T	I		A	M	I	E		S	E	T	S
R	U	N	I	N		B	O	O	S		T	R	I	O
K	N	O	C	K	A	B	O	U	T		R	I	L	L
S	I	N		B	L	E	D		I	C	I	C	L	E
			B	L	A	S		A	M	O	K			
C	E	L	L	O	S		T	R	A	D	E	W	A	R
E	L	I	O	T		H	I	R	T		F	A	T	A
S	L	O	W		H	E	N	I	E		O	L	A	V
A	I	N	T		O	A	T	S		F	R	E	R	E
R	E	S	O	U	N	D	S		T	O	C	S	I	N
			R	T	E	S		L	O	R	E			
P	R	I	C	E	Y		I	O	T	A		D	U	E
R	I	C	H		P	U	N	C	H	B	O	A	R	D
A	L	O	E		O	R	C	A		I	C	I	N	G
Y	E	N	S		T	E	A	L		T	A	S	S	E

67

C	A	P	P		M	A	A	M		S	P	A	K	E
O	D	O	R		O	U	R	S		W	A	N	L	Y
M	U	S	E		O	N	E	S		A	L	G	E	R
B	E	T	T	E	R	T	O		E	T	A	L	I	I
		P	E	A			L	I	G	H	T	O	N	E
A	L	O	N	G	S		A	D	O	S	E			
C	A	N	D	L	E		E	L	I		S	P	A	N
I	L	E		E	C	O		E	S	S		E	L	O
D	A	D	E		R	U	E		T	H	A	N	T	O
			S	P	E	C	K		S	A	V	I	O	R
C	U	R	S	E	T	H	E			N	E	T		
U	S	H	E	R	S		D	A	R	K	N	E	S	S
R	U	I	N	S		A	O	K	I		U	N	I	T
D	A	N	C	E		N	U	I	T		E	C	T	O
S	L	O	E	S		E	T	N	A		S	E	E	P

68

G	O	D		B	U	B	B	A		S	N	E	A	K
R	A	E		Y	P	R	E	S		T	E	R	R	E
A	T	M		D	E	A	T	H		R	U	I	N	G
S	H	O	T	I	N	T	H	E	D	A	R	K		
			A	N	D	S			A	D	O			
	L	A	S	T	S		B	A	L	A	N	C	E	D
R	A	T	S	O		S	E	L	A			A	R	E
O	U	T	O	F	T	H	E	P	I	C	T	U	R	E
A	R	I			R	A	P	S		R	U	S	E	S
R	A	C	E	W	A	Y	S		R	A	T	E	D	
			R	E	M			A	U	N	T			
		S	N	A	P	D	E	C	I	S	I	O	N	S
H	O	T	E	L		A	G	E	N	T		P	I	T
A	N	E	S	T		M	A	T	E	O		E	N	E
T	E	N	T	H		A	D	O	R	N		N	E	W

69

J	A	I	L		E	S	P	O	S	A		A	T	L
A	I	D	E		S	T	O	R	A	G	E	F	E	E
P	R	O	D	U	C	I	N	G	X	R	A	T	E	D
E	E	L		P	O	L	E				T	O	N	G
			S	O	R	T		I	M	M	E	N	S	E
A	C	C	E	N	T		S	L	O	A	N			
L	O	A	M			M	A	O	R	I		M	A	S
M	O	V	I	E	S	I	S	N	O	D	O	U	B	T
S	T	Y		M	E	N	S	A			P	L	E	A
			M	I	N	D	Y		C	H	E	E	S	Y
I	N	S	E	R	T	S		A	R	A	N			
P	A	T	E				A	M	U	R		H	A	Y
A	R	I	S	Q	U	E	B	U	S	I	N	E	S	S
S	C	R	E	E	N	T	E	S	T		E	R	I	E
S	S	S		D	E	A	L	E	Y		W	E	A	R

70

J	I	L	T		C	A	I	R	D		S	O	O	T
A	L	O	E		O	L	D	I	E		P	E	N	A
M	E	G	A		S	A	I	D	J	U	L	I	E	T
	T	O	R	O	M	E	O		E	T	A	L	I	I
			O	N	O			I	C	E	S			
I	F	Y	O	U		W	O	N	T	S	H	A	V	E
D	R	U	M	S		R	A	T	E			L	I	L
L	I	C	S		P	O	K	E	D		D	I	A	L
E	T	C			O	N	E	R		A	R	E	N	A
R	O	A	D	S	I	G	N	S		L	E	N	D	S
			E	E	N	S			C	S	A			
A	L	B	E	R	T		G	O	H	O	M	E	O	
B	U	R	M	A	S	H	A	V	E		S	A	M	S
E	R	I	E		T	I	L	E	S		U	T	A	H
T	E	E	D		O	P	E	N	S		P	A	N	E

71

B	A	C	H		C	H	I	C			S	H	A	G
A	S	I	A		H	A	S	H		S	K	I	L	L
S	H	A	N	G	R	I	L	A		P	U	L	S	E
				R	O	G	E	R		E	L	T	O	N
S	A	L	A	A	M			M	E	A	L			
P	R	E	M	I	E	R	E		C	R	I	S	I	S
A	M	A	I	N		E	T	C	H		S	E	N	T
R	U	N	T		Y	A	H	O	O		L	A	V	E
T	R	E	Y		E	R	I	C		P	A	G	A	N
A	E	R	I	A	L		C	O	R	O	N	A	D	O
			S	U	L	U			A	D	D	L	E	S
S	T	I	L	T		M	A	R	N	I				
H	A	G	A	R		B	R	I	G	A	D	O	O	N
I	R	O	N	Y		R	U	D	E		O	R	L	Y
N	A	R	D			A	G	E	D		C	O	D	E

72

Q	U	A	F	F	S		J	A	Z	Z		A	B	S
U	P	R	O	O	T		O	B	O	E		L	A	C
E	S	S	E	N	E		C	O	R	R		I	T	O
				D	R	E	A	D	N	O	U	G	H	T
R	A	P	T		E	L	S	E		M	A	N	E	T
I	N	R	E	V	O	L	T		L	O	W			
A	G	O	R	A		E	A	S	E	S		T	I	M
L	E	X	I	C	O	N		A	S	T	A	I	R	E
S	L	Y		U	P	S	E	T		E	L	M	E	R
			C	U	T		Q	U	I	L	T	I	N	G
E	P	S	O	M		P	U	R	R		I	D	E	E
S	H	O	O	T	B	L	A	N	K	S				
S	A	C		U	R	A	L		I	T	A	L	I	C
A	S	K		B	A	I	L		N	A	M	E	L	Y
Y	E	S		E	D	D	Y		G	R	A	T	E	D

73

A	W	E	D				M	A	O		O	S	I	P
L	O	V	E	L	Y		A	S	P		D	E	M	I
B	R	O	C	A	S		T	H	E	B	E	A	R	S
S	N	E	A	K	E	R		E	R	I	T	R	E	A
			P	E	R	I	L		A	G	T	S		
B	O	S	O	M		G	I	G		S	A	T	I	E
A	C	A	D	I	A		N	O	A	H		O	L	D
R	A	U		C	H	I	C	A	G	O		W	I	N
E	L	L		H	A	L	O		E	U	R	E	K	A
R	A	B	B	I		K	L	M		L	U	R	E	S
		E	E	G	S		N	E	E	D	S			
V	U	L	G	A	T	E		D	R	E	S	S	E	R
I	L	L	I	N	O	I	S		G	R	I	E	V	E
A	N	O	N		O	R	A		O	S	A	G	E	S
L	A	W	S		L	E	X				N	A	S	T

74

S	I	Z	E		S	L	E	W		S	E	M	I	S
E	R	I	K		T	O	N	O		P	L	E	A	T
C	A	P	E	V	E	R	D	E		R	I	D	G	E
				O	N	E	S			I	X	I	O	N
	A	C	T	I	O	N		C	O	N	I	C		
S	N	A	I	L	S		C	H	A	G	R	I	N	
A	G	R	E	E		L	A	I	R	S		N	O	R
G	O	D	S		W	E	L	D	S		M	E	T	E
S	R	I		E	A	G	L	E		C	O	H	A	N
	A	G	E	N	D	A	S		T	A	B	A	R	D
		A	N	G	E	L		C	R	U	S	T	Y	
H	E	N	R	I			W	O	O	S				
U	R	B	A	N		N	E	W	J	E	R	S	E	Y
S	T	A	G	E		A	R	E	A		A	P	S	E
K	E	Y	E	S		T	E	R	N		M	A	S	S

75

Y	A	N	G		C	A	P	S		C	H	A	S	M
A	M	O	R		A	D	U	E		H	A	D	T	O
R	O	T	I		L	I	R	A		A	N	Z	A	C
D	I	A	L	M	F	O	R	M	U	R	D	E	R	
			L	A	S	S			R	O	Y			
B	E	D	E	C	K		A	W	N		M	A	T	E
O	L	A		A	I	S	L	E			E	N	O	S
M	I	N	D	O	N	E	S	P	S	A	N	D	Q	S
B	A	K	E			M	O	T	E	T		R	U	E
E	S	E	L		Z	I	P		D	O	N	E	E	S
			T	A	O			M	U	L	E			
	E	F	O	R	E	X	C	E	L	L	E	N	C	E
A	V	A	I	L		R	O	L	O		D	A	U	B
V	E	R	D	E		A	L	O	U		E	Z	R	A
G	R	O	S	S		Y	E	N	S		D	I	E	N